CAMPING SURVIVAL HANDBOOK

CAMPING SURVIVAL HANDBOOK

ISBN: 978-1-942825-02-9

Author: Kambiz Mostofizadeh

Publisher: Mikazuki Publishing House

Copyright: 2015. All Rights Reserved.

Date Published: January 11th, 2015

Description: The Camping Survival Handbook is a manual for surviving and enjoying the wilderness.

No part of this work may be reproduced or transmitted in any form or by any means, electronic or mechanical, including photocopying, recording or by any information storage and retrieval system, without written permission from the publisher.

Like us on Facebook

www.facebook.com/bookspublishing

CAMPING SURVIVAL HANDBOOK

TABLE OF CONTENTS

Introduction - 3

The Mindset - 4

Proper Equipment - 9

Building a Fire - 17

Building Shelter - 26

Outdoor Cooking - 33

Star Gazing - 45

Dealing With Animals - 90

General Wilderness Rules – 92

Animal Tracks – 97

Draw a Map - 101

Making Knots - 103

Notes - 106

CAMPING SURVIVAL HANDBOOK

INTRODUCTION

Surviving and enjoying yourself in the wilderness is a great American pastime that has been practiced since the inception of America. The great pioneers and explorers like John Muir that trekked through the rugged American outdoors experienced many things that they shared with future generations. The adventurer spirit is woven in to the fabric of American culture and it started in the naked wilderness under the stars. I have spent the majority of my childhood camping throughout Northern and Southern California. I was a proud Boy Scout and greatly enjoyed every minute that I spent gazing at constellations and hiking through rocky creeks. This book is the sum of my theoretical and practical knowledge camping and surviving in the wilderness.

CAMPING SURVIVAL HANDBOOK

THE MINDSET

"Our outfit consisted of two yoke of oxen costing $117.50, a wagon costing about $80.00, our bedding consisting of buffalo robes and blankets, about 600 pounds of provisions, consisting of sacks of flour, one barrel of hardtack, a few boxes of Boston biscuit, some bacon, coffee, sugar, dried apples, etc. cooking utensils, two revolvers and a rifle."

- *William Smedley (1862)*

The proper mindset of a person that seeks to survive in the wilderness should be that of a person who is courageous, flexible, resilient, resourceful, and determined. Surviving in the wilderness is not easy but nor is it difficult. It depends on knowledge and the experience to be able to practice that knowledge. Part of the proper mindset is courage. Without courage, resilience and determination can hardly be enacted. Courage is therefore a key element for the camper. You may not know what is

CAMPING SURVIVAL HANDBOOK

behind the tree in the pitch dark night but you know that behind the tree there exists wood. Do you venture past the tree to find wood knowing that there is a small chance that there may be a bear waiting to attack you? That is where courage plays a key role. Flexibility is important for the camper because in the wilderness, things do not always go as planned. By being flexible, the camper saves his energy by not allowing circumstantial events to alter his mindset. The events cannot be controlled by the camper but he has to understand that they can be shaped. Resourcefulness plays a key role as well because the camper may not always have the right materials and will have to improvise to reach success. Being determined in camping means to know beforehand what you want accomplish and stay on the path until you have achieved it. You wouldn't leave a fire half started and you wouldn't build a shelter half way through and abandon it, would you? Of

CAMPING SURVIVAL HANDBOOK

course not. Resilience is part of the camping equation and involves your ability to "roll with the punches" or to "weather the storm" or not allow setbacks to deter you from your goal. Resilience, flexibility, resourcefulness, and determination make up the formula that creates the proper mindset for the modern camper seeking to survive and enjoy the wilderness. The following list will help to prepare the proper mindset and assist you in camping survival.

1. Be Positive and stay hopeful
2. Know your strengths and weakness'
3. At all times be realistic and honest with yourself about the situation you are in.
4. Identify issues and problems in order to deal with them.
5. Don't panic when you are in an unfamiliar situation.
6. Be patient for opportunities (food, shelter, water, items that will assist you, etc.)

CAMPING SURVIVAL HANDBOOK

7. Be aware of your surroundings at all times.
8. Stay Focused. Don't waste your physical or mental energy on issues unrelated to your goal.

WHAT IS SURVIVAL?
According to the United States Military survival stands for:

S - Size up the situation, surroundings, physical condition, equipment.

U - Use all your senses

R - Remember where you are.

V - Vanquish fear and panic.

I - Improvise and improve.

V - Value living.

A - Act like the natives.

L - Live by your wits.

CAMPING SURVIVAL HANDBOOK

BEFORE YOU START YOUR JOURNEY

1. Give at least two individuals information as to the location you will be camping in. These two people can help find you if you do not come back in time.

2. Notify these two individuals of the length of your camping trip.

3. Pack only things you need and avoid extra items. The less you carry in the wilderness, the faster you can travel.

4. Take Waste Disposal bags to properly separate your trash so as to not harm the wilderness.

5. Don't assume technology will work in the wilderness. Self-sufficiency is the most important quality in the wilderness.

CAMPING SURVIVAL HANDBOOK

PROPER EQUIPMENT

"We need the tonic of wildness. At the same time that we are earnest to explore and learn all things, we require that all things be mysterious and un-explorable that land and sea be indefinitely wild, un-surveyed and unfathomed by us because unfathomable. We can never have enough of nature."
— Henry David Thoreau

The proper equipment is vital for a safe and enjoyable venture in to the wilderness. There are a base set of items that any camper should have and then are the secondary items which ensure a safe trip for the camper.

The following items are the Main Items:

1. **Matches**
    Reason: Light fire

CAMPING SURVIVAL HANDBOOK

The best type of matches are waterproof matches and/or matches that can be lit on any surface.

What You Should Know: The more matches you pack, the more assured you will be in your camping adventure. The fire is the most vital element to a safe and enjoyable camping trip. It will warm you, cook your food, and keep pesky critters away from your campsite.

2. **Warm Clothing**

    Reason: Stay warm

    The ideal clothing for camping is clothing that contains wool. Avoid synthetic fabrics and seek natural fibers. Multiple layers assists in keeping warm as do thickly knit socks

    What You Should Know: It is better to be warm than to be cold when you are in the outdoors. Be generous when packing clothes.

CAMPING SURVIVAL HANDBOOK

3. **Tent**

    Reason: Shelter

    The ideal tent is a tent that takes little space, is light enough to carry, and is made of a fabric that can provide adequate warmth.

    What You Should Know: When buying a tent, ask for a tent has the capability of keeping you alive in zero degree temperature.

4. **Sleeping bag**

    Reason: Provides a comfortable place of rest and provides additional warmth The ideal sleeping bag is both lightweight and able to provide proper comfort.

    What You Should Know: Pick the sleeping bag that can withstand the lowest temperature.

CAMPING SURVIVAL HANDBOOK

5. **Flashlight**

   Reason: Visibility

   The ideal flashlight is compact and uses LED lighting. A solar waterproof flashlight can be of great importance when batteries fail.

   What You Should Know: A flashlight that fails in action can be quite disappointing. Check the batteries and turn on each flashlight before taking them with you. LED flashlights give the most luminescence. Waterproof flashlights are ideal for times when you are wading through a flowing creek.

6. **Water Canteen**

   Reason: Carry drinking water

   The ideal canteen is small, attached to the waist or back, and can carry at least 1 liter of water.

   What You Should Know: Water conservation is among the important

CAMPING SURVIVAL HANDBOOK

elements in outdoor survival. To quote Frank Herbert in his legendary book Dune "Water is life."

7. **Swiss Army Knife**

    Reason: Multiple purpose knife for being able to cut wood and other associated uses.

    The ideal Swiss Army Knife contains different edged blades so as to be adaptable to various situations in the wilderness.

    What You Should Know: Swiss Army Knives come in all different sizes and varieties. Pick the one that has the most utility.

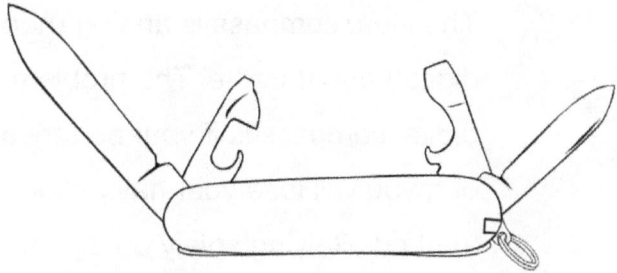

CAMPING SURVIVAL HANDBOOK

8. Gloves

Reason: Protect your hands from cuts during picking firewood and to keep your hands warm.

The ideal gloves have a warm soft interior with a rough durable exterior.

What You Should Know: Gloves that protect your hands are most vital because the last thing you will want is to visit the hospital three hours away for stitches because you have cut your hand on a jagged broken branch.

9. Compass

Reason: Location identification and route navigation

The ideal compass is analog (non-digital) and durable. The problem with a digital compass is if your batteries run out, you will lose your navigation method. Relying solely on digital navigation weakens your overall skills in

CAMPING SURVIVAL HANDBOOK

being able to navigate without digital devices.

What You Should Know: An analog compass is one of the oldest and the most important tool for navigation. Learn to use it and familiarize yourself with its workings.

10. **Backpack**

    Reason: Storing and carrying tent, sleeping bag, and Secondary Items. The ideal backpack is large enough to carry your main items and has a frame so as to not hurt your back when carrying heavy loads.

    What You Should Know: A backpack's exterior looks are important but the utility and ability to carry heavy loads while reducing tension on the body differentiate between mediocre and superior backpacks.

CAMPING SURVIVAL HANDBOOK

11. **Candles**

    Reason: Your flashlight may fail and you may need to resort to candles for lighting.

    What You Should Know: Buy waterproof candles or outdoor candles.

By packing and being skilled in the use of the eleven items mentioned, you will be able to have a safe and enjoyable camping trip. The key is to understand the importance of each and their functions.

CAMPING SURVIVAL HANDBOOK

BUILDING A FIRE

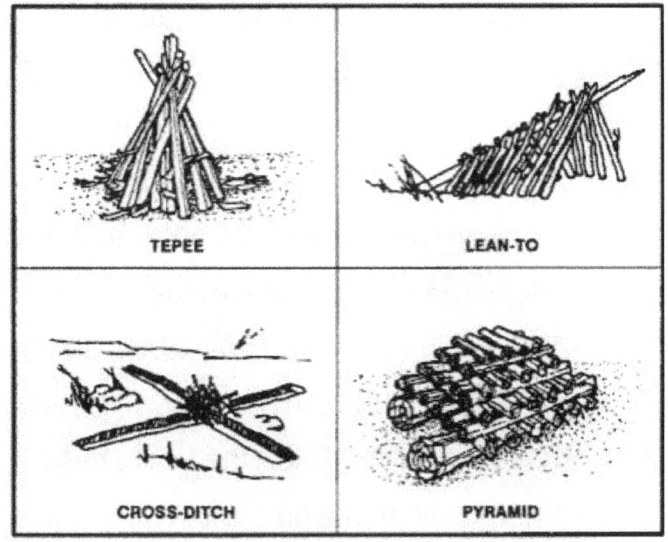

    The fire is the centerpiece of your camping trip and it is the most important element in your camping trip. The fire will provide a source of entertainment for you as well as warming and cooking your food. Additionally the fire assists in keeping unwanted animals away from your campsite. The keys to building a good fire are the following:

   1. Gathering Firewood

CAMPING SURVIVAL HANDBOOK

When gathering firewood, you want to search and gather as much dead wood as you can. What is dead wood? Dead wood is wood that has fallen from a tree and has become dried up. It is "dead" meaning that it is no longer a part of the living organism called the tree. This is the most useful for burning because it is dry. Dead wood can be found wherever there are trees. Under the trees, there are usually an assortment of different sizes of deadwood waiting to be gathered.

CAMPING SURVIVAL HANDBOOK

2. Building a Fire Pit

In order to build a fire, you must have an enclosure in which to build the fire in. This enclosure should be a round or square formation of rocks. These rocks are placed in a square or circle formation in order to create a perimeter around the fire preventing the fire from going out and allowing the fire to condense thereby growing stronger. Even stones should be gathered making the rock perimeter known as the fire pit. The fire pit should be no bigger than 50 centimeters by 50 centimeters. This will allow the coal (made from the burning of wood as the wood transforms to hot coal) to gather efficiently allowing your fire to grow stronger.

3. **Lighting the Fire**

First you must a small amount of leaves and place it in an open formation (don't

CAMPING SURVIVAL HANDBOOK

block the wind flow between the leaves!) in the fire pit. Pick up one leaf and light it up with your matches. Use this leaf to light the leaves you have placed in an open formation in the fire pit. Keep placing leaves and small sticks until the fire grows a little larger. Now place larger sized sticks over the smaller sticks to keep the fire growing. The fire is built in layers and it is the placement of leaves, small sticks, and larger sticks that creates the hot coals necessary for placing a log (a large piece of wood) on the fire. There are elements necessary for building a proper fire and they are:

a. Following the Sequence
First you must place and light dry leaves, place small sticks onto them, place larger sticks on them, and then place logs on to the fire. This is the proper sequence to be followed and

CAMPING SURVIVAL HANDBOOK

attempting to re-invent the wheel when building a proper fire will result in delayed enjoyment. The sequence is simple but must be followed. Leaves ->Small Sticks->Mid-Size Sticks->Large Sticks->Logs

b. Proper Placement
The sticks should be placed in an X like formation to allow the necessary amount of air to travel under the fire causing the fire to keep growing. A fire depends on air and that is why windy conditions not only do not stop a fire but they do quite the opposite, they build the fire. Throwing a heavy log on to sticks without allowing air flow between the log and the sticks, will kill the fire. There has to be airflow between the log and the sticks to allow the log to burn. Then sticks should be fed in between the

CAMPING SURVIVAL HANDBOOK

log and the burning coals below it. Feeding the fire and building it depends on proper placement.

The fire pit will be the center of your campsite and a place to gather around for meals, talk, and general enjoyment. A well-built fire pit with properly placed wood can give 4-5 hours of warmth and content.

IF YOU ARE WITHOUT MATCHES

If your matches have run out, there are still a few methods available to you.

Ice Lens

In the movie The Edge, Anthony Hopkins explains to a distraught Alec Baldwin that you can make fire from ice. It is indeed true that ice can be molded in to a lens and used to magnify the rays of the sun.

CAMPING SURVIVAL HANDBOOK

Friction Method

By rubbing a harder piece of wood against a softer piece of word, you are able to generate friction that result in creating sparks.

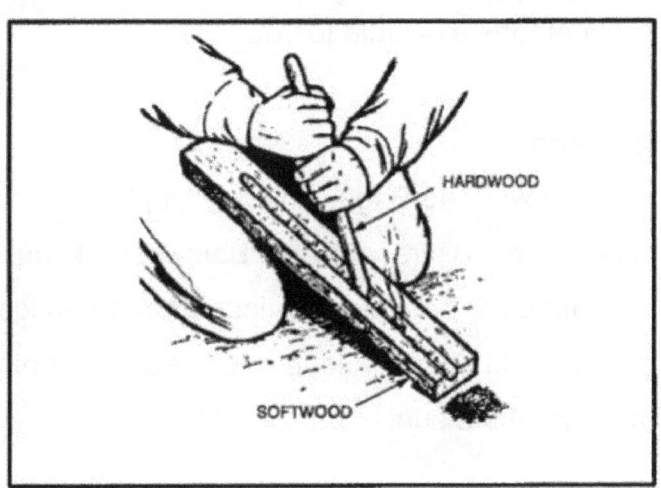

CAMPING SURVIVAL HANDBOOK

With each movement of the stick back and forth, both wood shavings are created and friction is generated. The wood shavings provide the tinder and the flame you need to create a fire. It is a difficult method and must be practiced in order to be executed under stressful conditions.

TINDER

Tinder is dry material that is gathered to light up. It is a dry material and the following items make good tinder:

    a. Dry Leaves

    b. Very thin dry sticks

CAMPING SURVIVAL HANDBOOK

BUILDING SHELTER

A shelter can protect you from the sun, insects, wind, rain, snow, and hot or cold temperatures. It can give you a feeling of well-being. It can help you maintain your will to survive.

In some areas, your need for shelter may take precedence over your need for food and possibly even your need for water. For example, prolonged exposure to cold can cause excessive fatigue and weakness (exhaustion). An exhausted person may develop a "passive" outlook, thereby losing the will to survive.

The most common error in making a shelter is to make it too large. A shelter must be large enough to protect you. It must also be small enough to contain your body heat, especially in cold climates. If you have a tent with you (as you should) then the tent is your shelter and your place of rest. If you do not have a tent with you, then there are a few methods for creating shelter.

CAMPING SURVIVAL HANDBOOK

CLEARING THE AREA

Before setting up your shelter, first you will have to clear the area. Clearing the area means that you should remove any debris, rocks, obstacles, or any objects in that area. The area should be no larger than three to four meters in diameter and it should be in an area that is clear of brush and vegetation. Sleeping on a wet surface will give you bodily pain and may result in even worse maladies. In addition, the area should be level as setting up a shelter on a slope can be a tricky proposition. You should avoid areas that are near water, near loose rocky slopes, or on vegetation.

Difficulty: Easy

Total Time: 15 Minutes

CAMPING SURVIVAL HANDBOOK

FIRST METHOD – A FRAME TENT

This is the simplest and fastest method for setting up shelter.

1. Pick a pair of trees 3-4 meters apart.

2. Take a piece of rope and extend it between two trees. Make sure the rope is drawn around the trunk of each tree and is firmly fastened by being tied in a knot. The elevation of the rope should be at least 200 centimeters. The rope serves as the skeleton for your shelter.

CAMPING SURVIVAL HANDBOOK

3. After the rope has been erected between the two trees, then use a large tarp or blanket to create your tent.

4. Use rocks to hold the side of the tents in place and to prevent movement. You can also use two long pieces of wood places in an X like formation to keep the tent from moving.

This is a fast and simple method that can be done alone.

Difficulty: Easy

Time Needed: 30 Minutes

Materials Needed:
Rope
Blanket
Heavy Rocks or 2 Long Sticks

SECOND METHOD – TEPEE

CAMPING SURVIVAL HANDBOOK

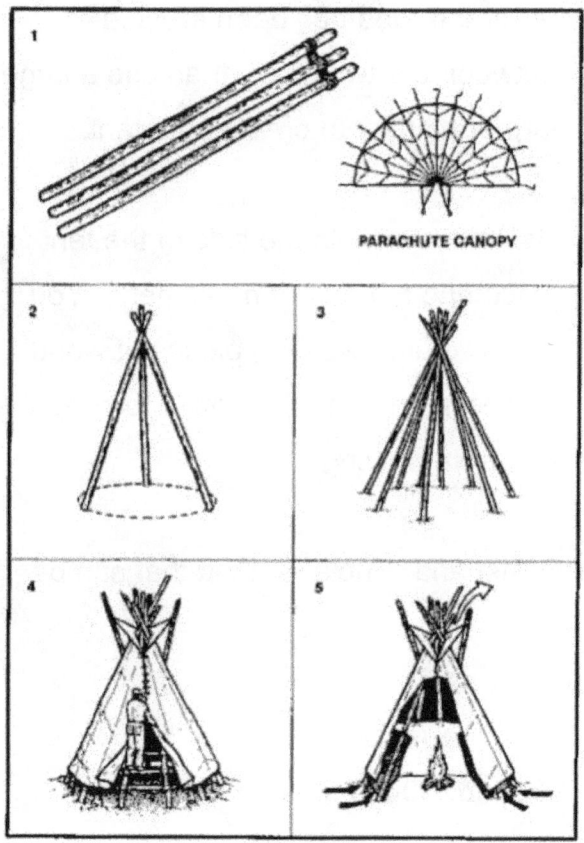

1. Gather 3 long pieces of wood, each about 2 meters in length.

2. Tie their tops together while they are on

3. Stand them up and pull the sticks apart until they are in a cone like formation.

CAMPING SURVIVAL HANDBOOK

4. Cover the exterior with fabric or vegetation.

5. Stitch the top and leave an opening for entering and exiting.

Difficulty: Easy

Time Needed: 30 Minutes

Materials Needed:
Rope
Blanket
Heavy Rocks or 2 Long Sticks

CAMPING SURVIVAL HANDBOOK

THIRD METHOD – LINE SHELTER

The line shelter is a simple and fast method for setting up a shelter for a single individual.

1. Take a rope and fasten one end of it around a tree at 1 meter height.

2. Fasten the other end of the rope around a large rock approximately the size of a volleyball or basketball.

3. Draw a tarp or fabric over the rope/line.

Difficulty: Easy

Time Needed: 15 Minutes

CAMPING SURVIVAL HANDBOOK

Materials Needed:

Rope

Blanket/Tarp/Fabric

1 Heavy Rocky

OUTDOOR COOKING

Among the greatest enjoyments when camping in the wilderness is outdoor cooking. If for whatever reason you are stranded in the wilderness without food, then you must be resourceful in order to survive. You will be able to source food in two ways:

    a. Gather Food – You will spend your time attempting to identify non-poisonous edible plants, vegetables, and leaves that you can eat to stay alive.

    b. Hunt for Food – You will spend your time creating traps, laying snares, and using makeshift weapons to capture your food.

CAMPING SURVIVAL HANDBOOK

For some people, option A is more realistic than option B. You may however be in a situation where option A is not workable and you will have to hunt for your food.

GATHERING FOOD
There are two ways to gather food when surviving in the wilderness and they are:
    a. Active Gathering
        1. Identifying non-poisonous edible plants and vegetables

        2. Gathering and storing them

        3. Preparing and/or cooking them

        4. Using their scraps (Be Resourceful)

    b. Passive Gathering
        1. Laying traps and snares

CAMPING SURVIVAL HANDBOOK

Laying traps and snares depends on creating simple mechanisms whereby you can capture your food.

BIRD TRAP

A simple trap is presented below, that you can construct from the same material used for making an A Frame Tent.

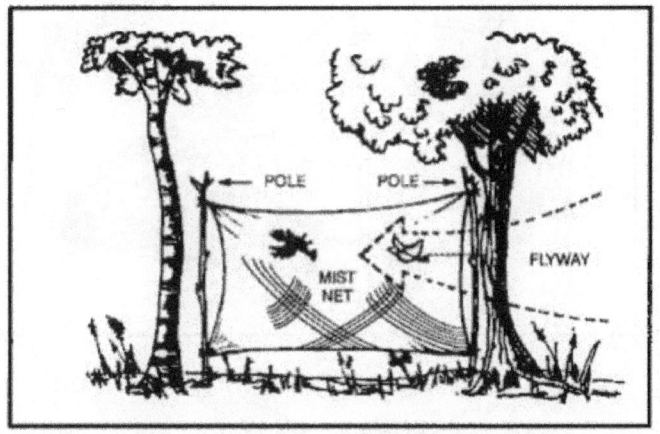

1. Find two trees no farther apart than 2-3 meters.

2. Use rope to bind each of the four corners of the tarp or fabric to each tree.

CAMPING SURVIVAL HANDBOOK

3. The birds are stunned when they hit the bird trap, giving you 5-10 seconds to capture the stunned bird.

DEADFALL
Paiute Deadfall

1. Find a boulder light enough to lift but heavy enough that it will crush a small animal.

2. Lift the rock and place a stick under the rock. The stick should be long enough so that a small animal could walk under it.

CAMPING SURVIVAL HANDBOOK

3. Place another stick at a diagonal angle to help prop up the rock.

4. Connect a piece of string, wire, or thin rope between the diagonal stick and the main stick propping up the rock.

5. Finally connect a long rope to the main stick propping the rock and await at a distance.

6. When a small animal enters under the trap, pull the string and recover your food! Also if an animal "trips" the wire/rope connecting the diagonal stick and the main stick, the trigger will be released and the rock will capture your food.

HUNTING UTENSILS

Hunting utensils are the tools used to kill an animal that you plan on eating. Hunting an animal should only be done when you have no food and you know you will starve if you do not find food. The most effective tools for hunting are the following:

1. Slingshot – Perfect for small game.

2. Rabbit Stick – Midsized spear as long as the human arm, made for throwing at small game.

3. Spear – Long stick with a sharpened end approximately the height of a human. Used for stabbing at mid to large sized game. Also can be used for fishing.

WHERE TO HUNT
Hunting should only be done as a last resort. If the choice is to starve or to hunt, it is better to hunt.
Watering Holes or wherever there is water to drink, animals will gather.

CAMPING SURVIVAL HANDBOOK

KEYS TO HUNTING

1. Use surprise

2. Be quiet in movement

3. If armed with a spear use single stabbing motions.

4. If armed with melee weapon like slingshot or rabbit stick, then take aim quietly and fire through your target.

5. Hunting is used as a last resort to prevent you as a human being from starving. A person that chooses to starve to death rather than hunt is not making a wise decision.

6. Be responsible and don't over-hunt. Just fulfill your needs to survive.

CAMPING SURVIVAL HANDBOOK

COOKING THE FOOD

Once you have caught your food, you must prepare it. The following steps should be taken with the game:

a. Skin it – You should skin the animal to prepare it for cooking.

b. Remove its head and/or entrails

c. Skewer it – Use a long thin but durable stick (that is sharpened on the entry end) to skewer the captured game.

CAMPING SURVIVAL HANDBOOK

BARBECUE GAME

Place the skewers over the fire at a distance that will prevent the food from burning but will allow a medium and thorough cooking to take place.

    a. Coal Building – Build up a considerable amount of hot coals and then spread them out in the fire pit (you should have created one!) to achieve a consistent heat pattern.

    b. Avoid Meat Over Flame – This will prevent the meat from cooking, will give an uneven heat pattern resulting in uncooked and cooked parts, and will

CAMPING SURVIVAL HANDBOOK

burn the exterior leaving an uncooked interior.

c. Seasoning – Use natural seasonings handpicked from leaves, flowers, and vegetation.

EDIBLE PLANTS

1. Grass – Can be boiled in to a soup or eaten raw.

2. Palm trees – They provide dates and coconuts

3. Cactus – Can be eaten raw or its pieces can be cooked.

4. Pine Cones – Pine nuts are edible within the pine cones on pine trees. Break open the pine cone and harvest the multiple seeds within in it. Can be eaten raw or cooked.

CAMPING SURVIVAL HANDBOOK

    5. Acorns – Must be roasted or boiled

PLANTS TO AVOID

    1. Three leafed plants

    2. Thorny plants (except Cacti)

    3. Plants with shiny leaves

    4. Plants with almond scent

    5. Plants with milky sap

    6. Umbrella shaped flowers

    7. Fungus

DEALING WITH POISON PLANTS
Skin irritants (includes poison oak and poison ivy).

(1) Wash with large amounts of water. Use soap (if available).

(2) Keep covered to prevent scratching.

CAMPING SURVIVAL HANDBOOK

DEALING WITH SNAKE BITES

(1) Nonpoisonous. Clean and bandage wound.

(2) Poisonous.

(a) Remove constricting items.

(b) Minimize activity.

(c) DO NOT cut the bite site; DO NOT use your mouth to create suction.

(d) Clean bite with soap and water; cover with a dressing.

(e) Overwrap the bite site with a tight (elastic) bandage. The intent is to slow capillary and venous blood flow but not arterial flow. Check for pulse below the overwrap.

(f) Splint bitten extremity to prevent motion.

(g) Treat for shock
(h) Position extremity below level of heart.

(i) Construct shelter if necessary (let the victim rest),

(j) For conscious victims, force fluids.

CAMPING SURVIVAL HANDBOOK

STAR GAZING

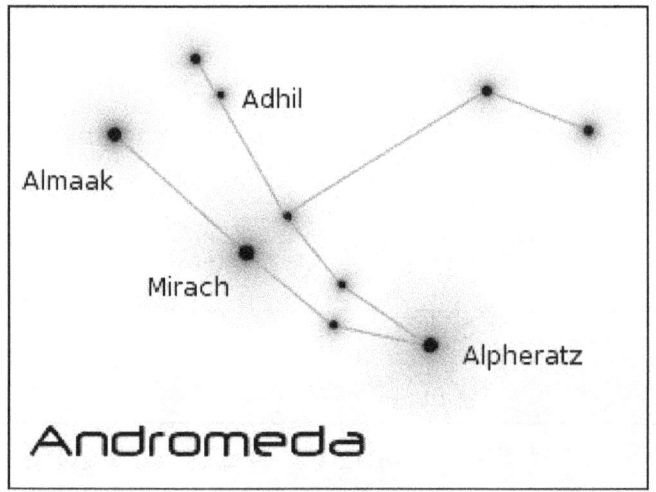

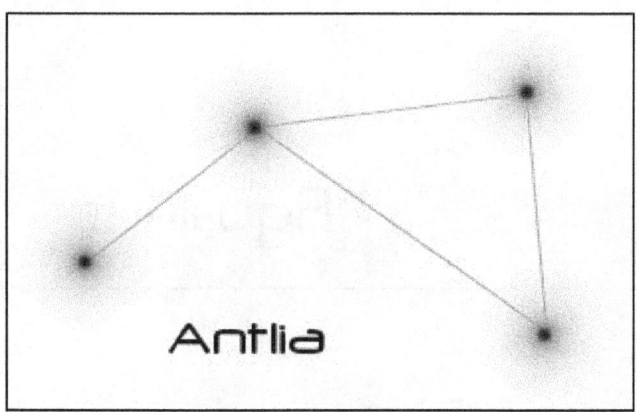

CAMPING SURVIVAL HANDBOOK

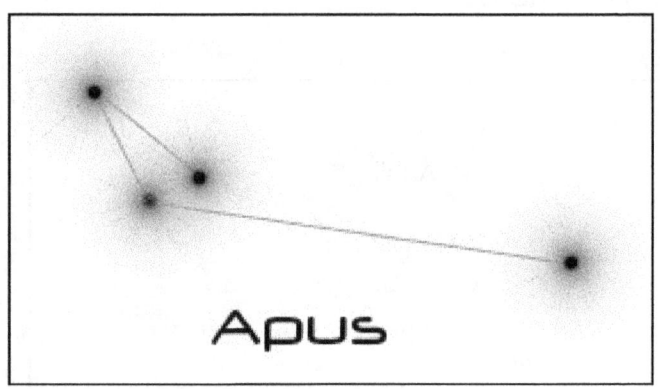

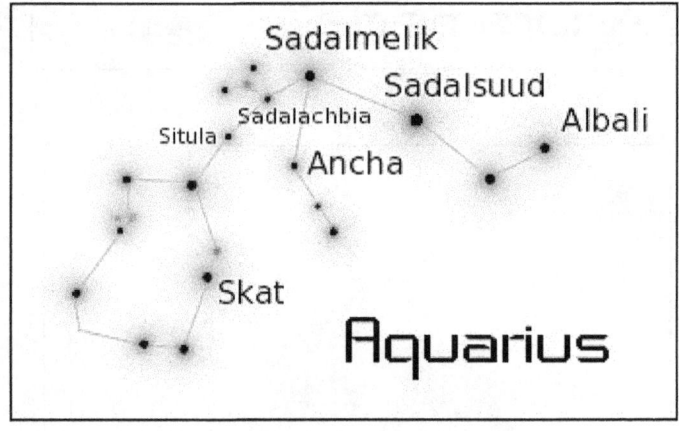

CAMPING SURVIVAL HANDBOOK

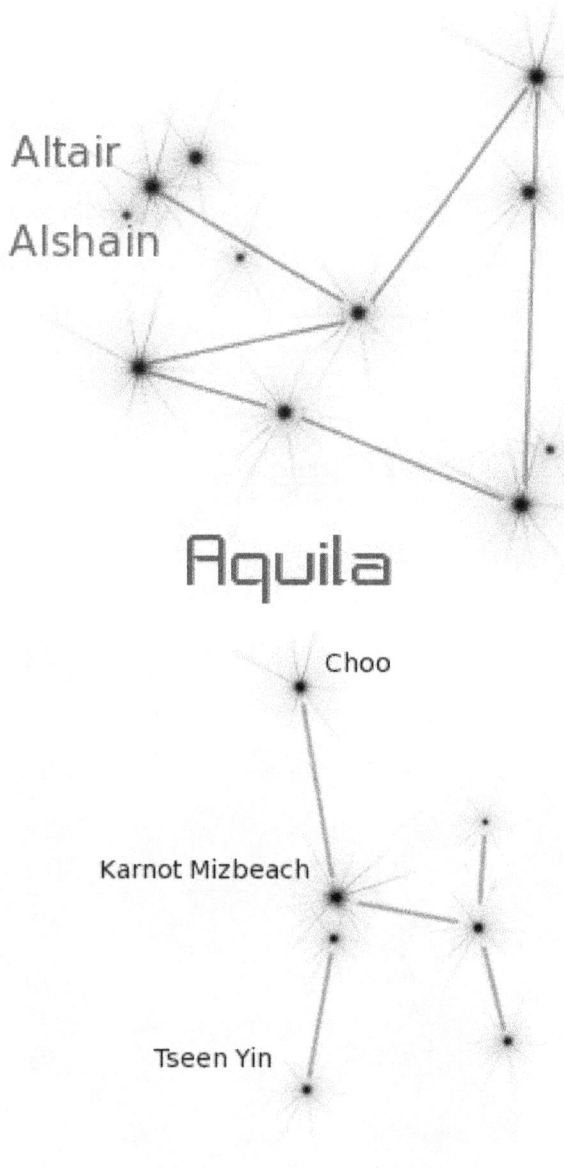

CAMPING SURVIVAL HANDBOOK

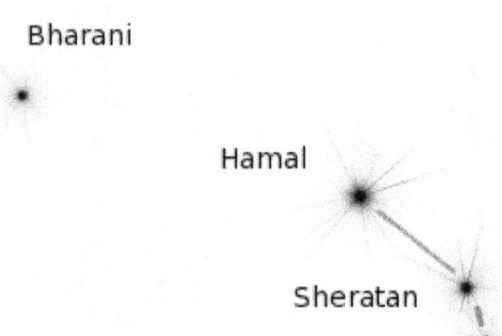

Aries

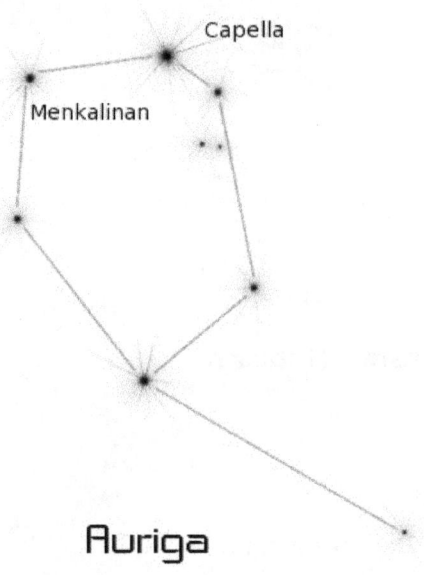

Auriga

CAMPING SURVIVAL HANDBOOK

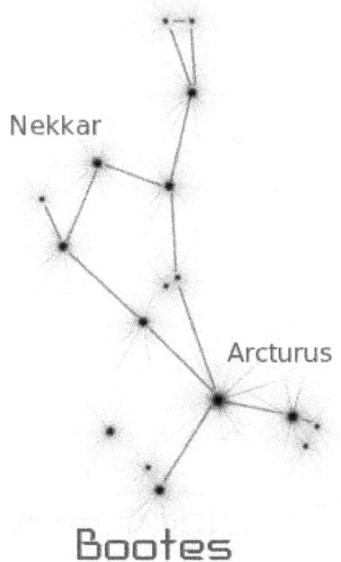

Bootes

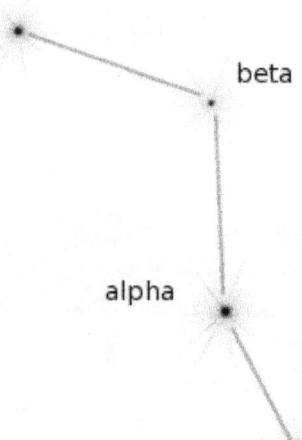

Caelum

CAMPING SURVIVAL HANDBOOK

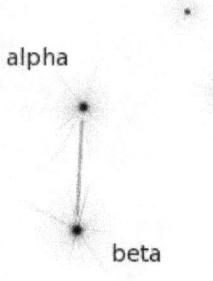

Camelopardalis

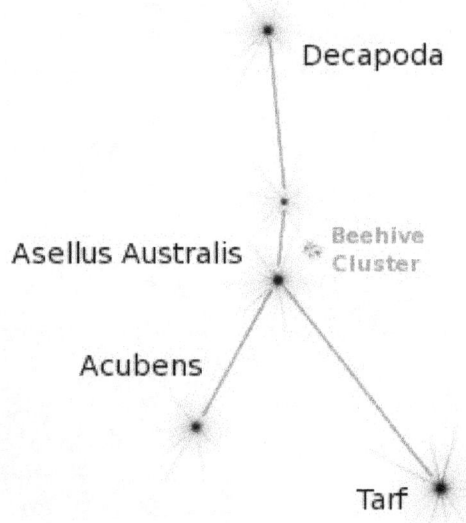

Cancer

CAMPING SURVIVAL HANDBOOK

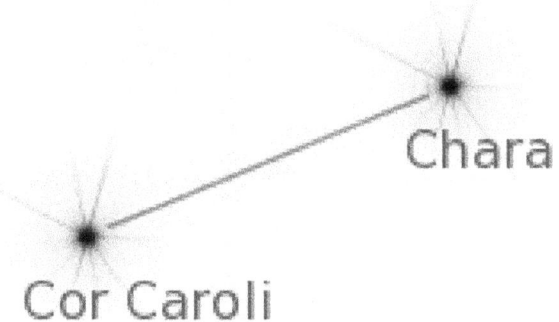

Canes Venatici

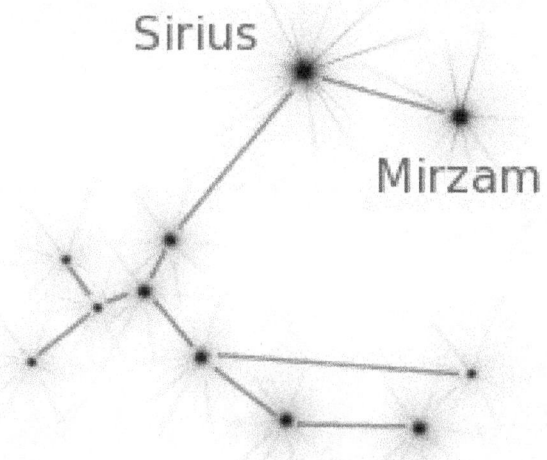

Canis Major

CAMPING SURVIVAL HANDBOOK

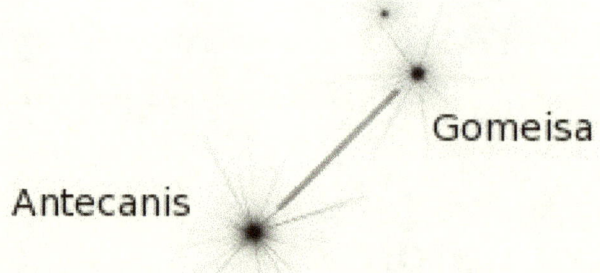

Canis Minor

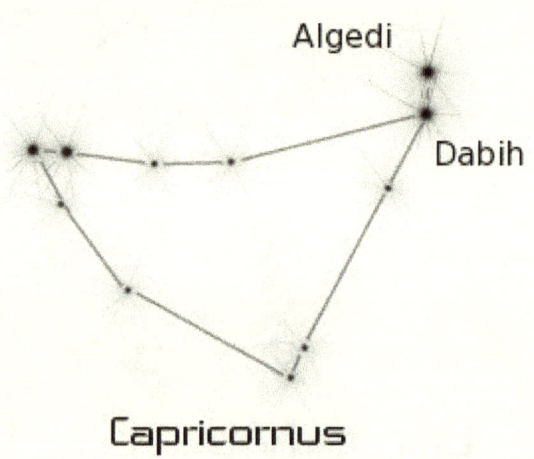

CAMPING SURVIVAL HANDBOOK

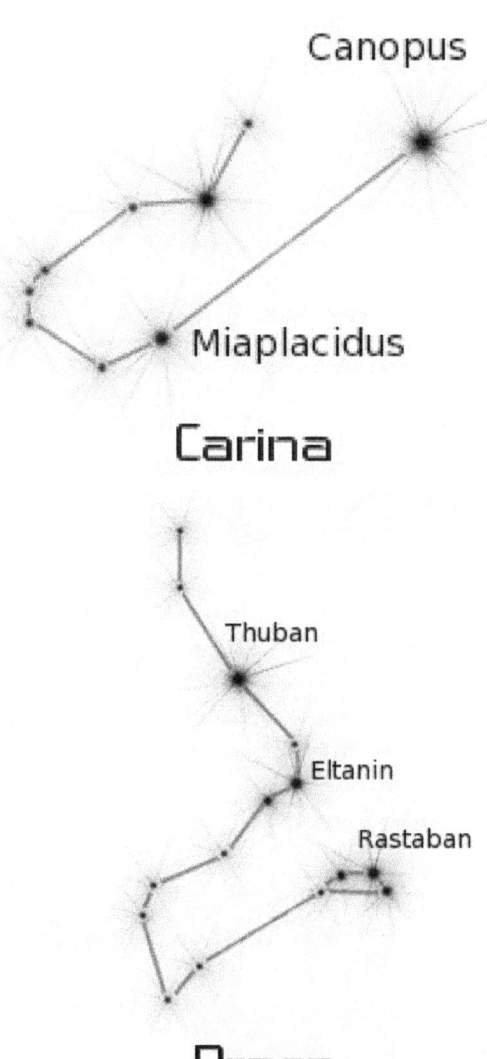

CAMPING SURVIVAL HANDBOOK

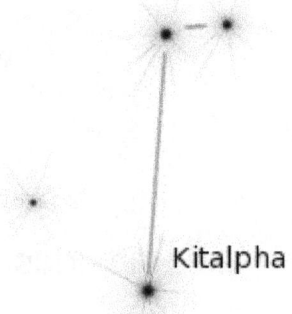

Pherasauval

Kitalpha

Equuleus

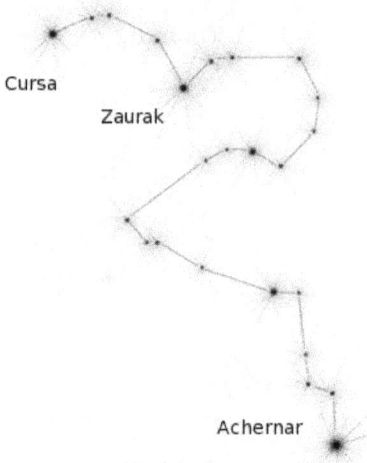

Cursa

Zaurak

Achernar

Eridanus

CAMPING SURVIVAL HANDBOOK

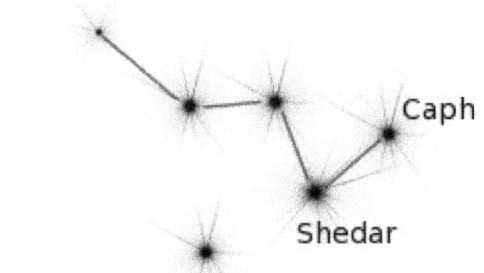

Cassiopeia

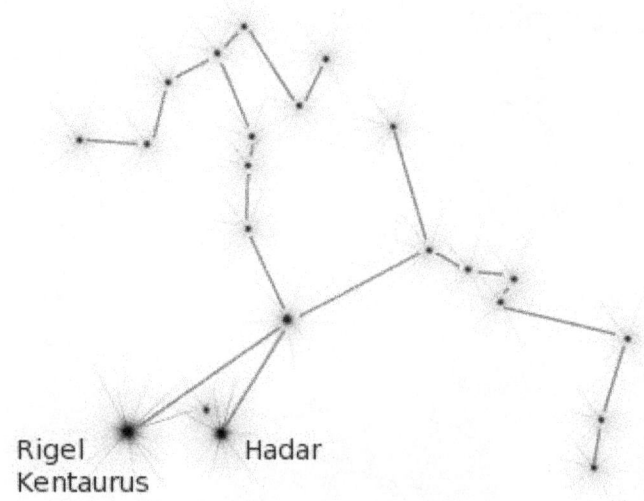

Centaurus

CAMPING SURVIVAL HANDBOOK

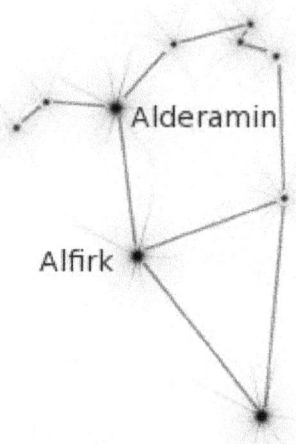

Cepheus

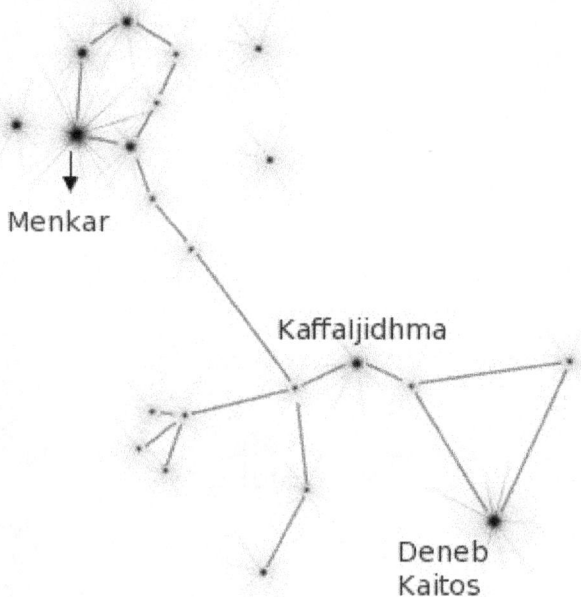

Cetus

CAMPING SURVIVAL HANDBOOK

Chamaeleon

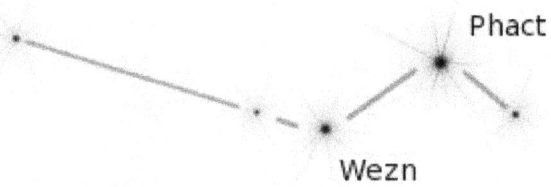

Columba

CAMPING SURVIVAL HANDBOOK

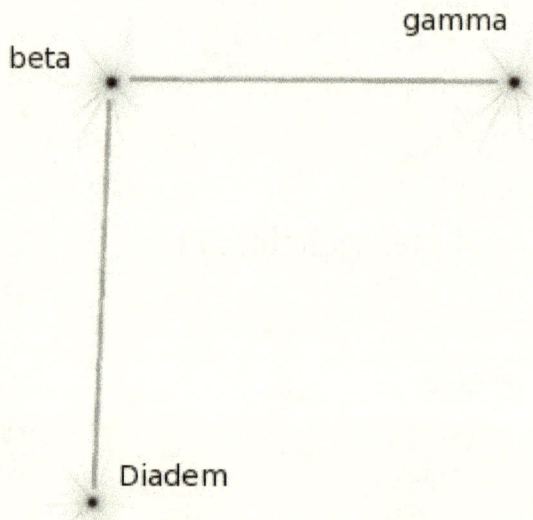

Coma Berenices

CAMPING SURVIVAL HANDBOOK

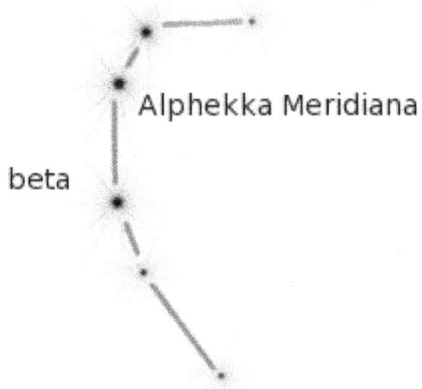

Corona Australis

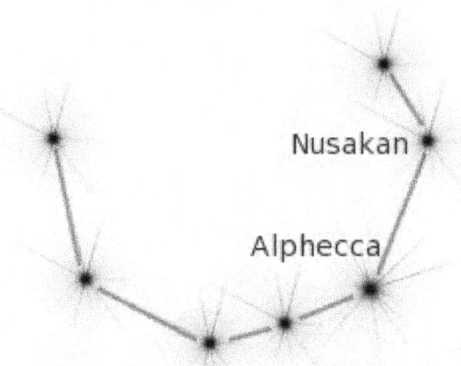

Corona Borealis

CAMPING SURVIVAL HANDBOOK

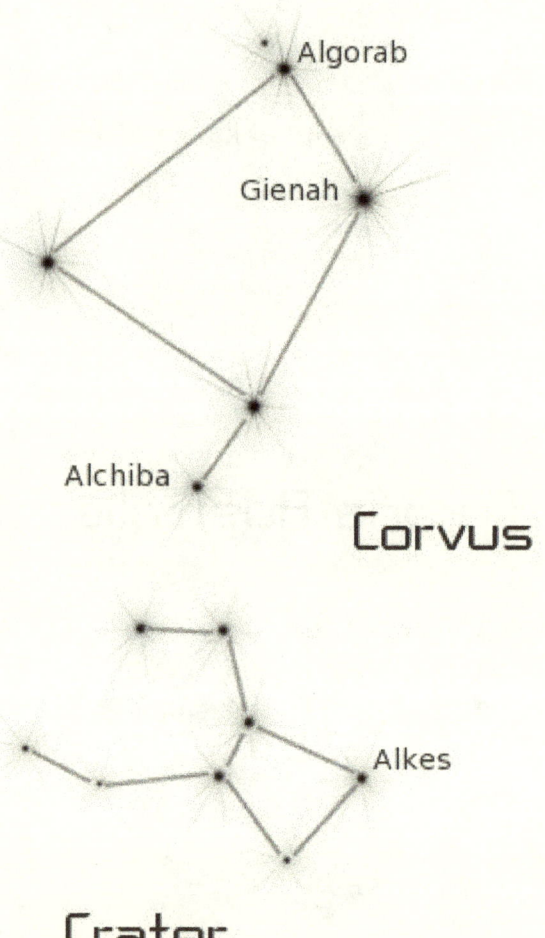

CAMPING SURVIVAL HANDBOOK

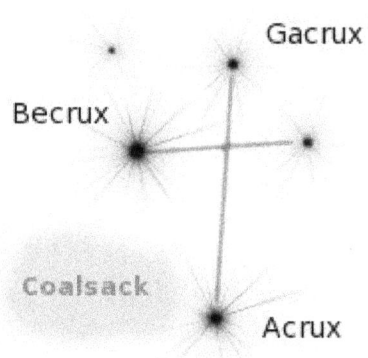

Crux

Cygnus

CAMPING SURVIVAL HANDBOOK

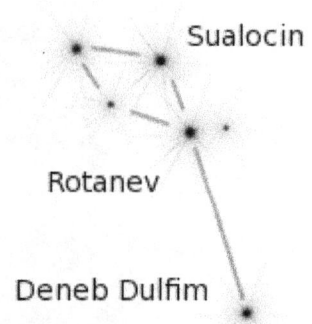

Delphinus

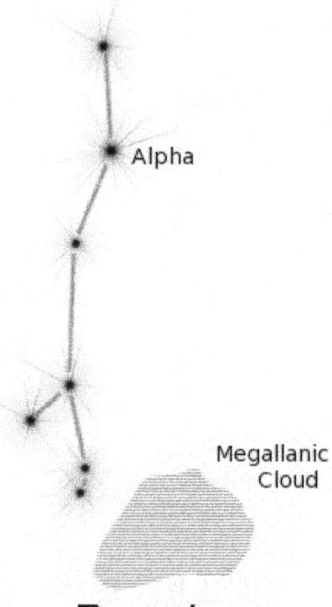

Dorado

CAMPING SURVIVAL HANDBOOK

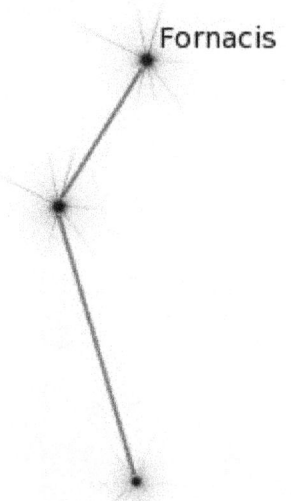

Fornax

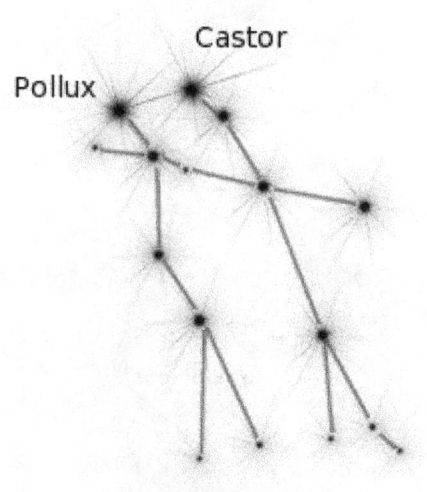

Gemini

CAMPING SURVIVAL HANDBOOK

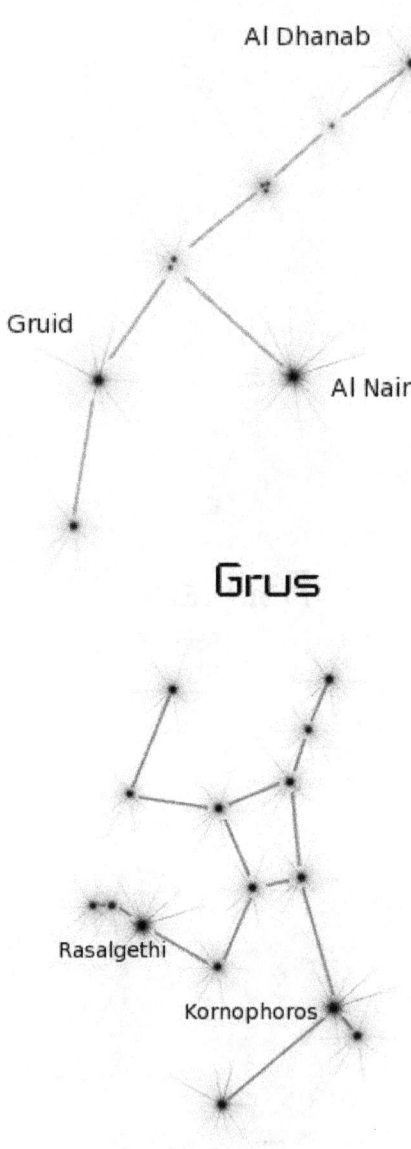

Grus

Hercules

CAMPING SURVIVAL HANDBOOK

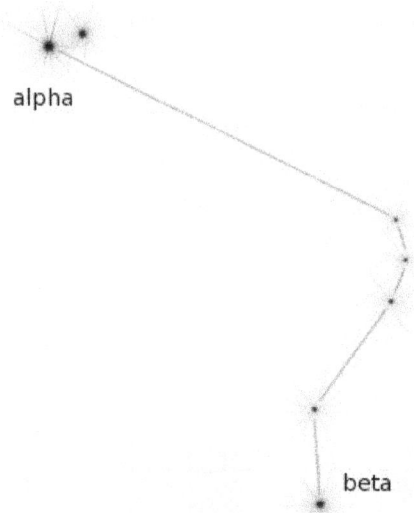

Horologium

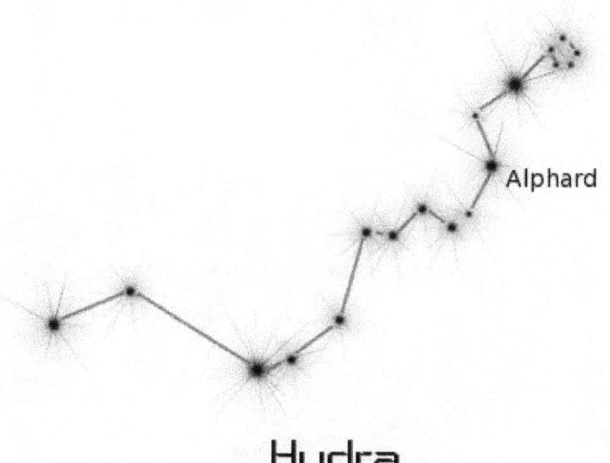

Hydra

CAMPING SURVIVAL HANDBOOK

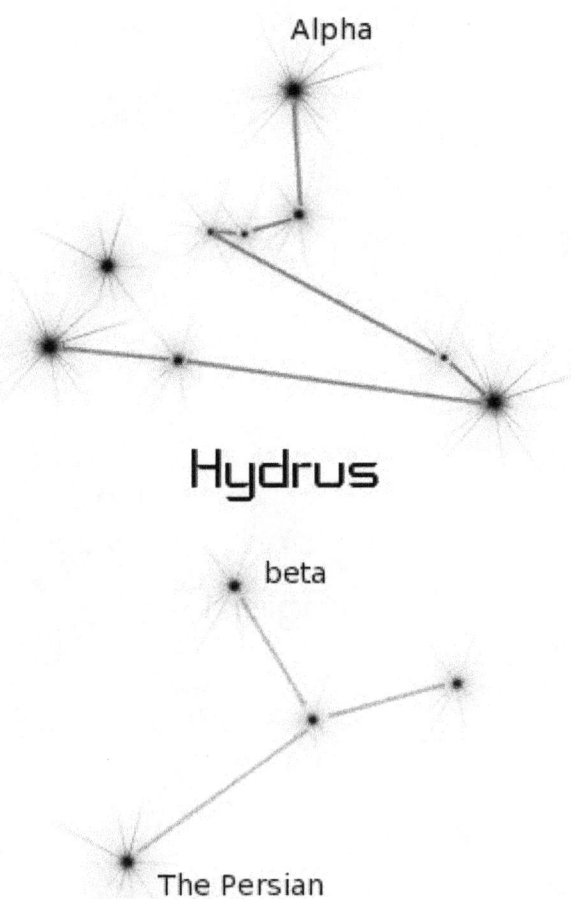

Alpha

Hydrus

beta

The Persian

Indus

CAMPING SURVIVAL HANDBOOK

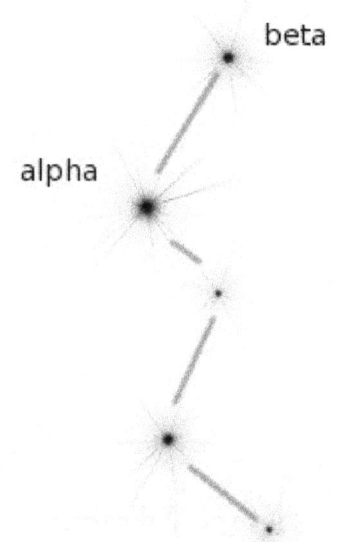

Lacerta

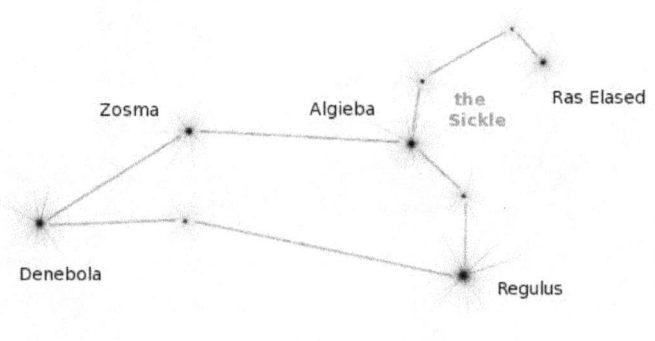

Leo

CAMPING SURVIVAL HANDBOOK

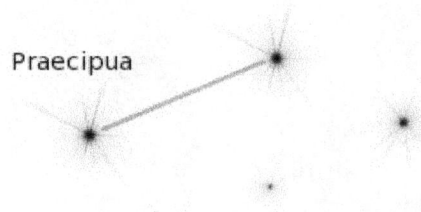

Leo Minor

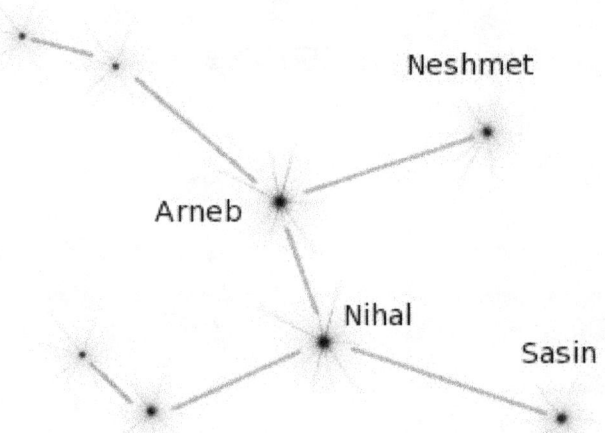

Lepus

CAMPING SURVIVAL HANDBOOK

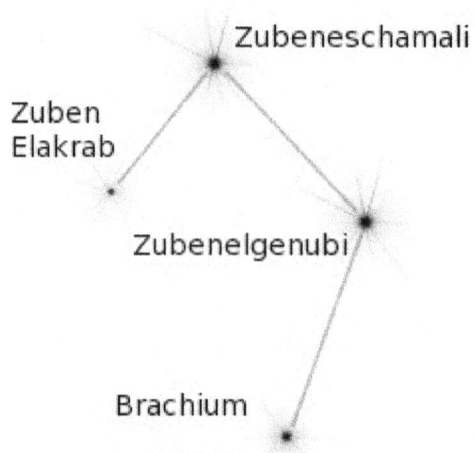

Libra

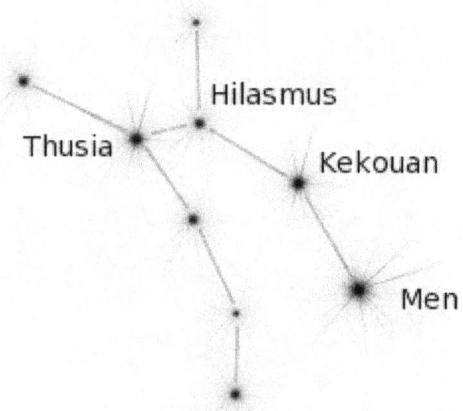

Lupus

CAMPING SURVIVAL HANDBOOK

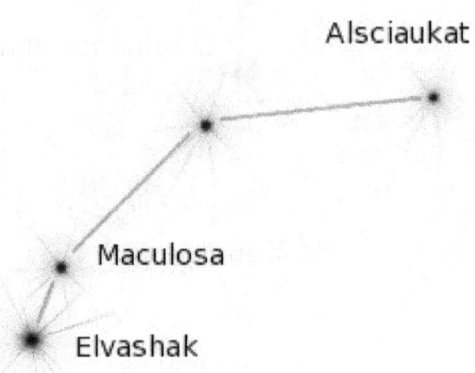

Lynx

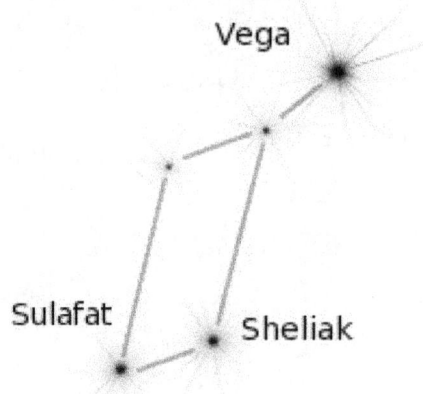

Lyra

CAMPING SURVIVAL HANDBOOK

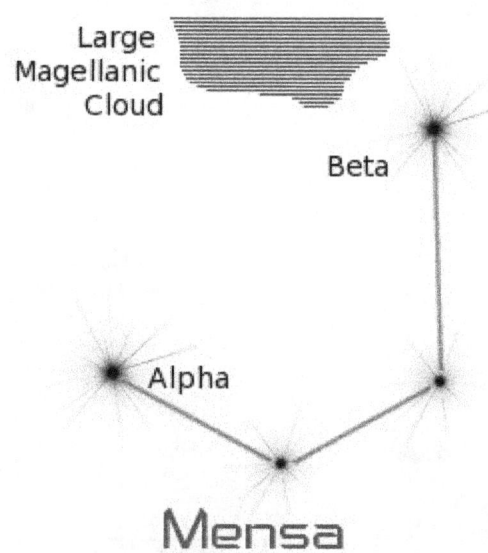

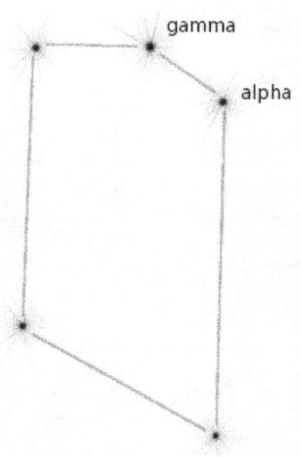

CAMPING SURVIVAL HANDBOOK

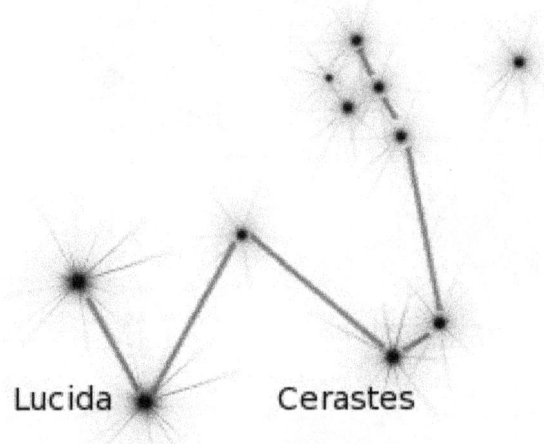

Monoceros

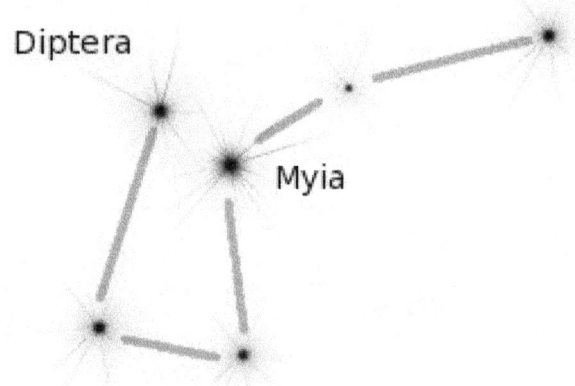

Musca

CAMPING SURVIVAL HANDBOOK

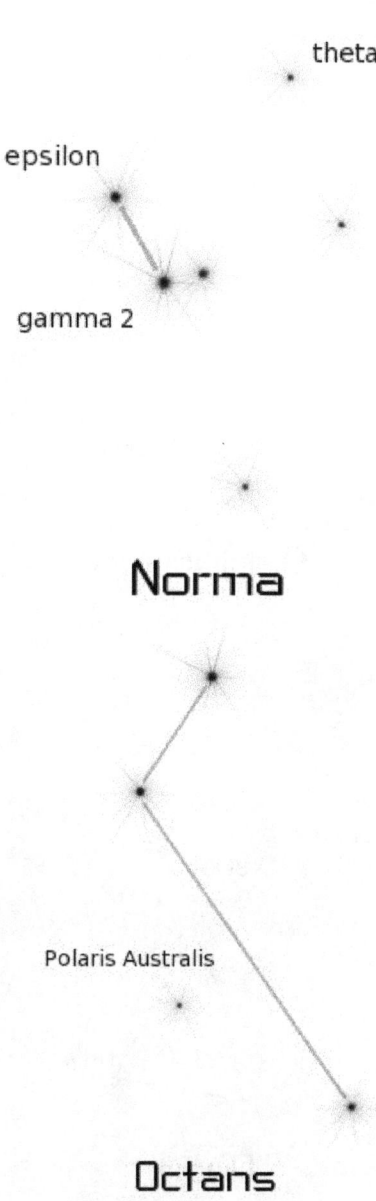

CAMPING SURVIVAL HANDBOOK

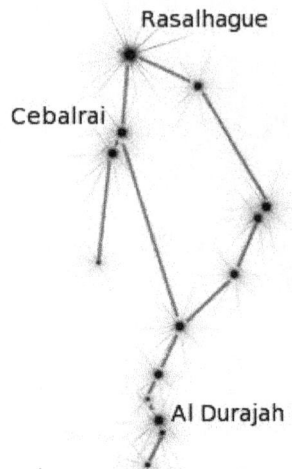

Ophiuchus

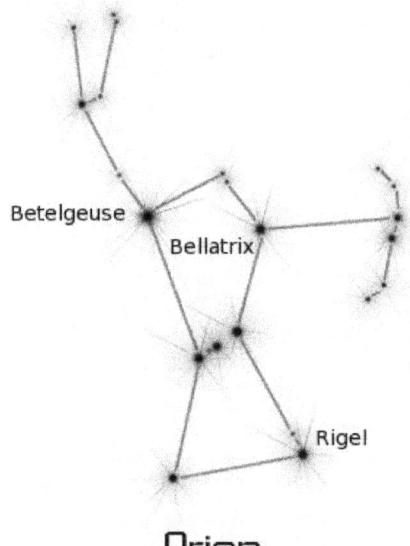

Orion

CAMPING SURVIVAL HANDBOOK

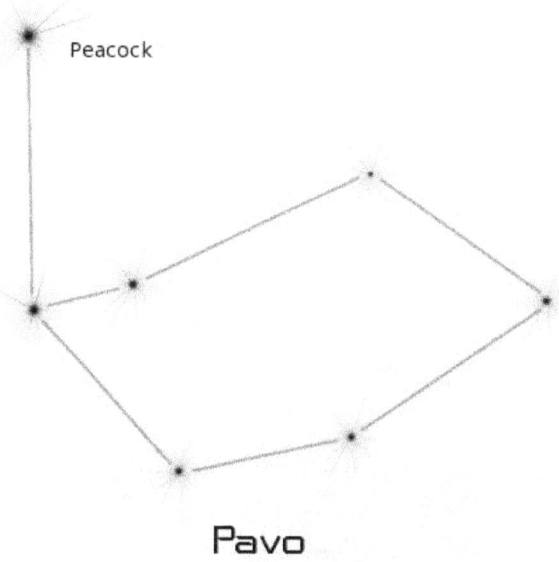

Pavo

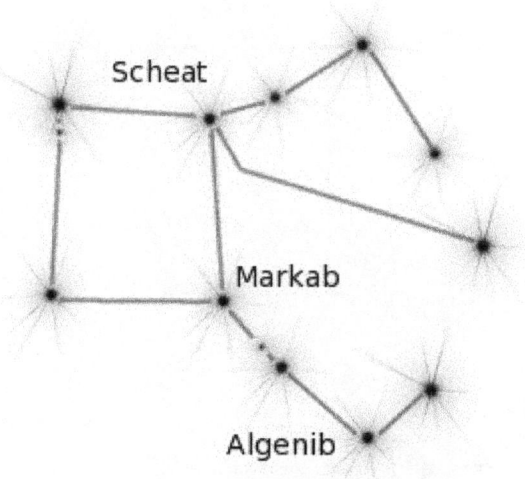

Pegasus

CAMPING SURVIVAL HANDBOOK

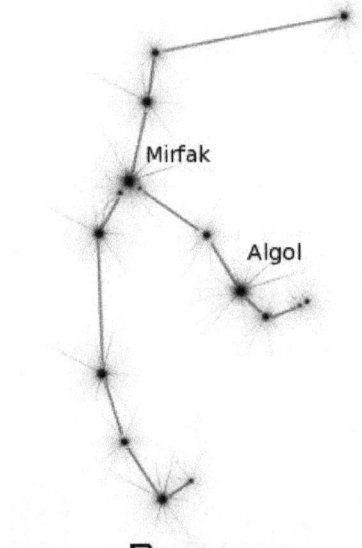

Perseus

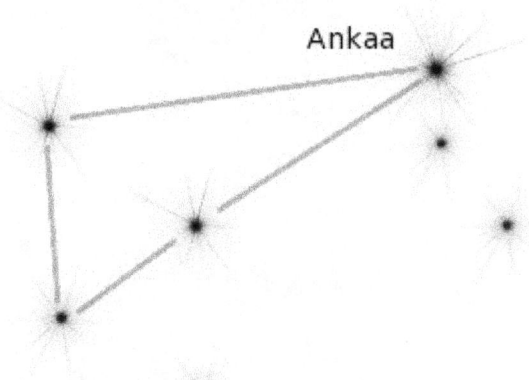

Phoenix

CAMPING SURVIVAL HANDBOOK

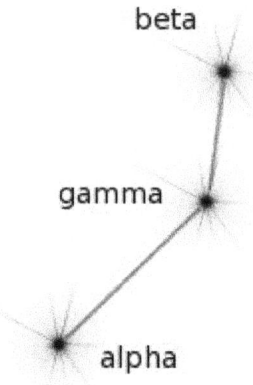

Pictor

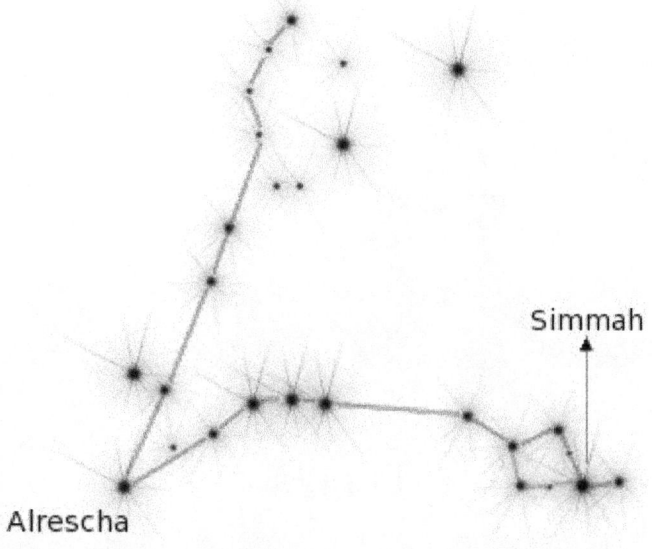

Pisces

CAMPING SURVIVAL HANDBOOK

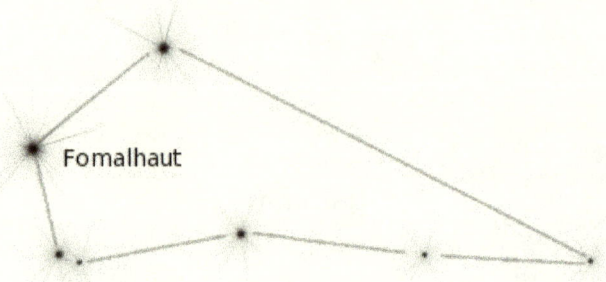

Piscis Austrinus

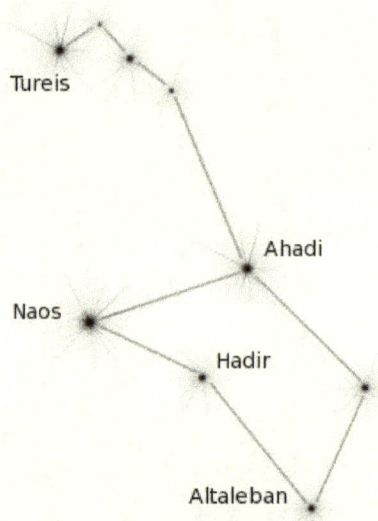

Puppis

CAMPING SURVIVAL HANDBOOK

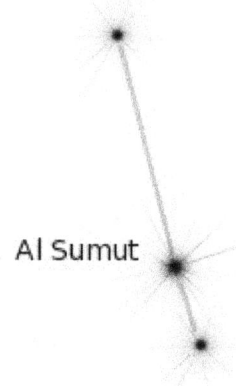

Al Sumut

Pyxis

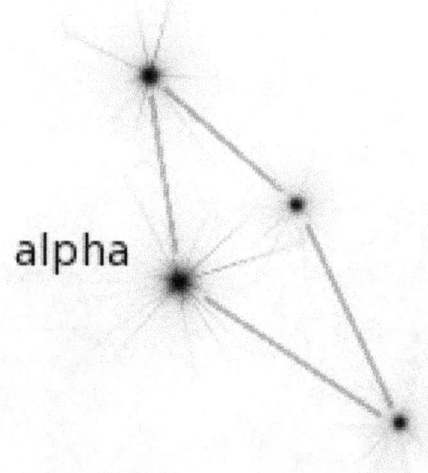

alpha

Reticulum

CAMPING SURVIVAL HANDBOOK

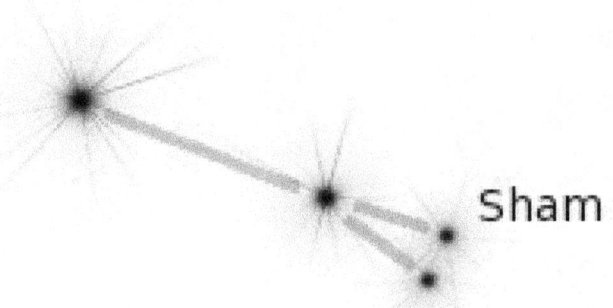

Sagitta

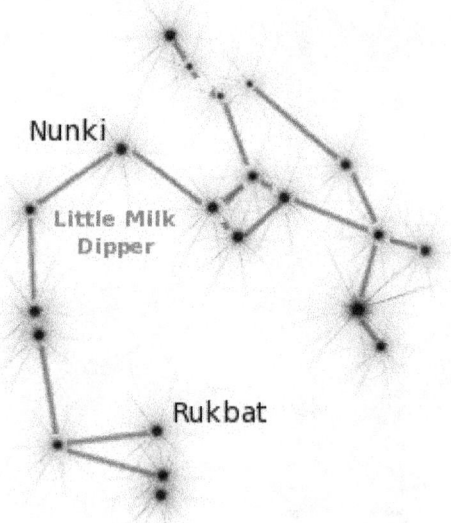

Sagittarius

CAMPING SURVIVAL HANDBOOK

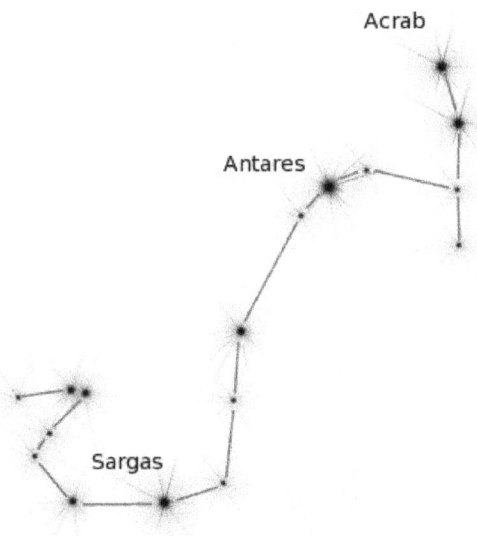

Scorpius

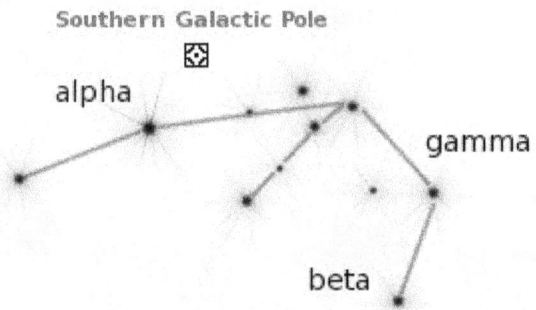

Sculptor

CAMPING SURVIVAL HANDBOOK

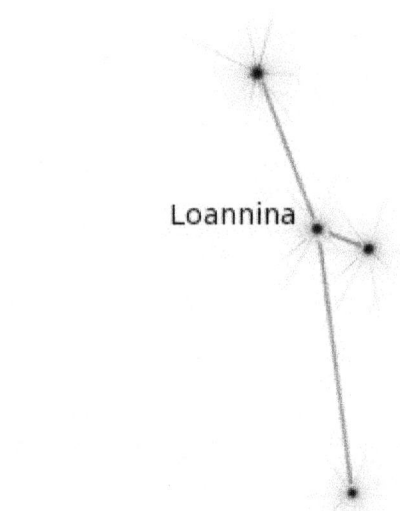

Scutum

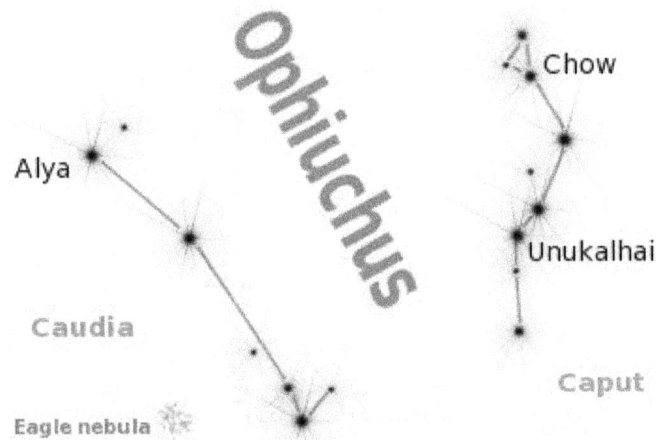

Serpens

CAMPING SURVIVAL HANDBOOK

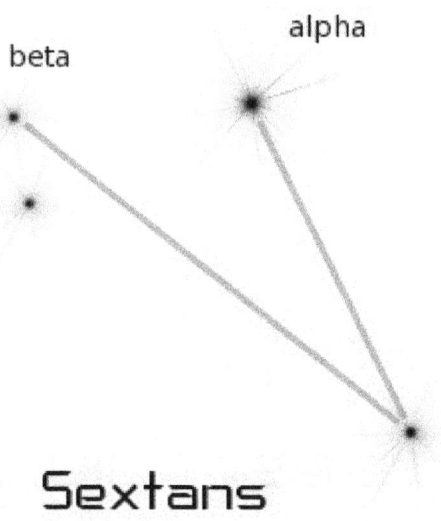

Sextans

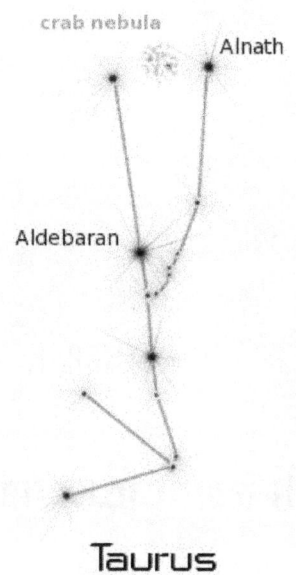

Taurus

CAMPING SURVIVAL HANDBOOK

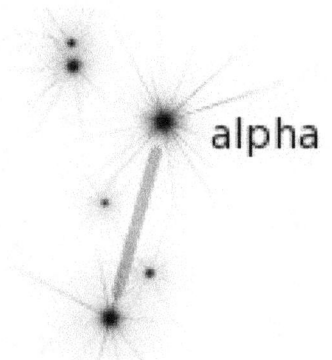

Telescopium

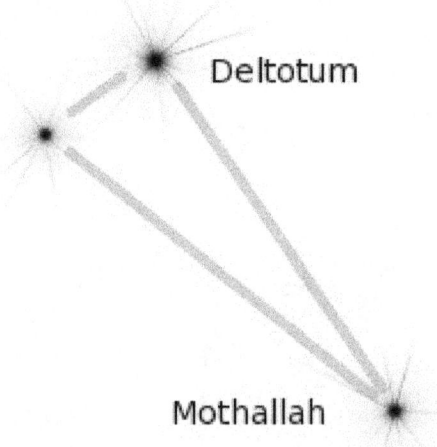

Triangulum

CAMPING SURVIVAL HANDBOOK

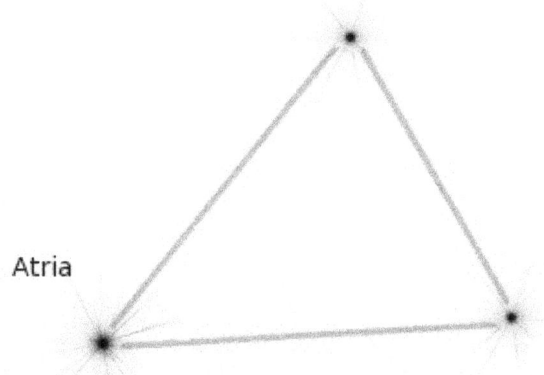

Triangulum Australe

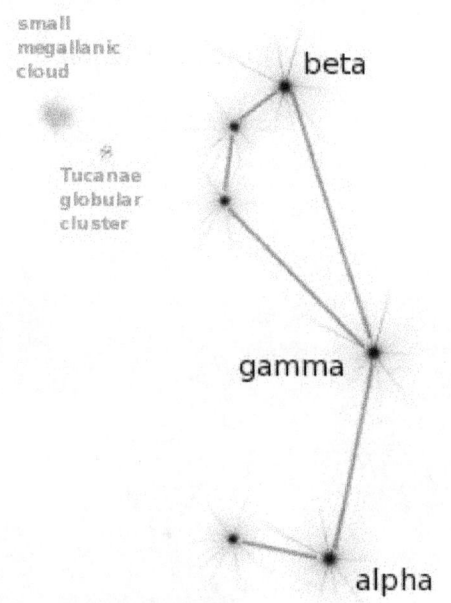

Tucana

CAMPING SURVIVAL HANDBOOK

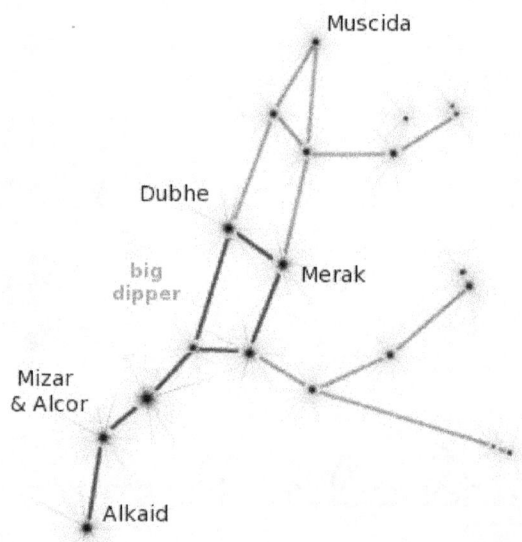

Ursa Major

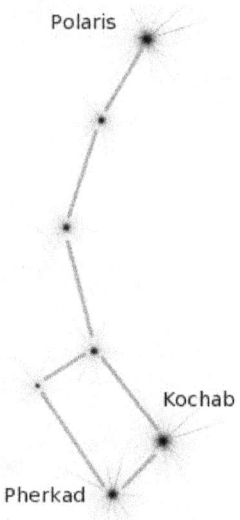

Ursa Minor

CAMPING SURVIVAL HANDBOOK

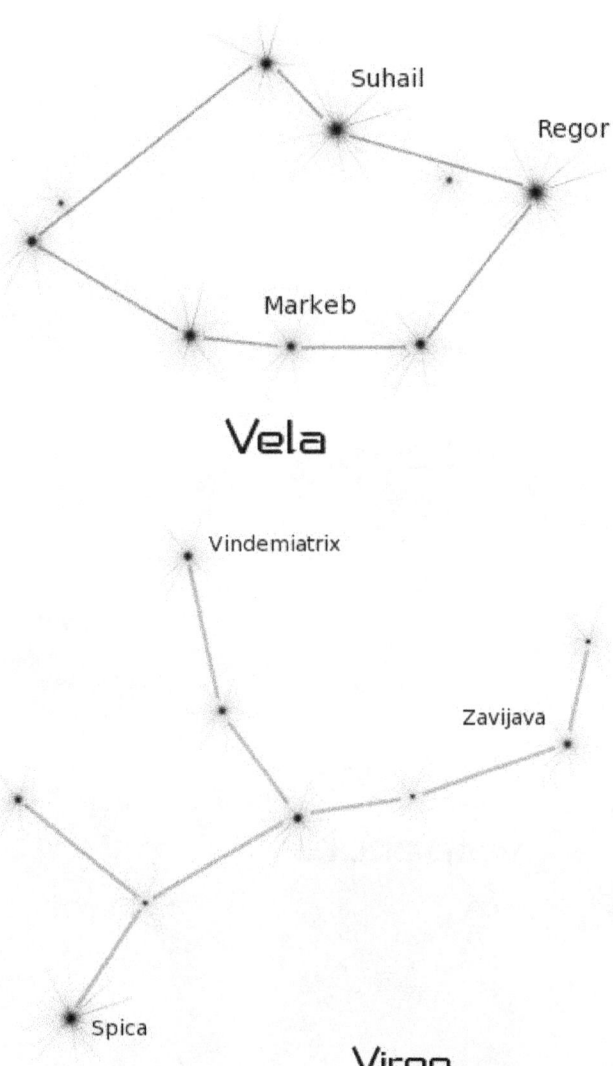

CAMPING SURVIVAL HANDBOOK

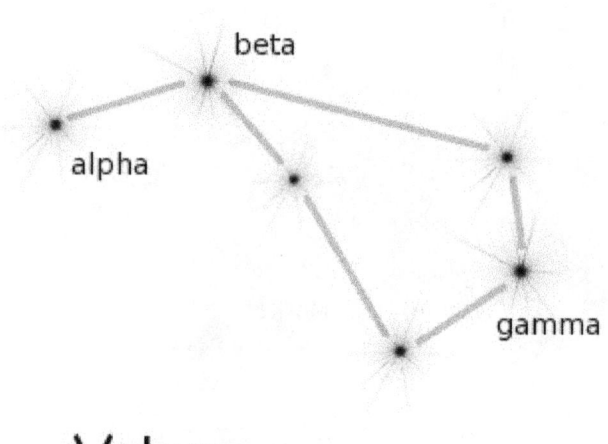

Volans

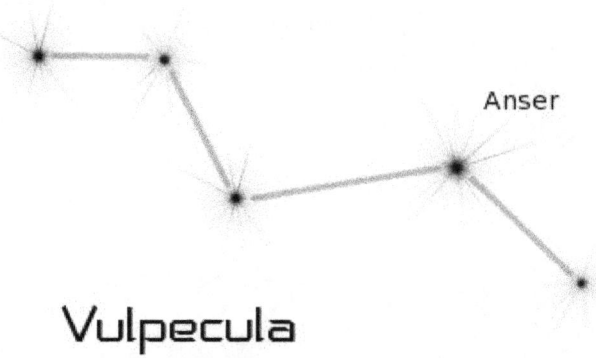

Vulpecula

CAMPING SURVIVAL HANDBOOK

NAVIGATE BY THE NORTH STAR
1. Find the Big Dipper Constellation

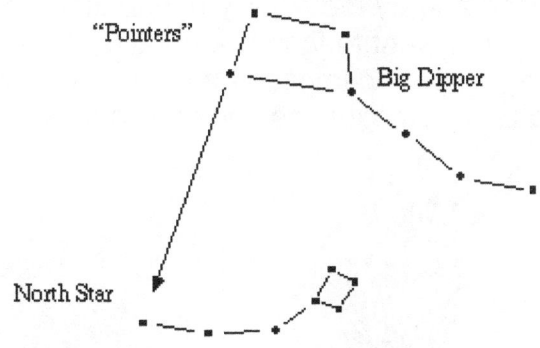

Source: UCLA

2. Using the Big Dipper, you can locate the North Star. Use the North Star to find the direction that you wish to travel.

3. Travel downstream to reach people and more hospitable conditions.

4. Travel at night for warmer conditions and easier movement.

CAMPING SURVIVAL HANDBOOK

DEALING WITH ANIMALS
Animals are many times attracted by the scent of food and by the activity of humans. The last thing you want to face is a hungry Black Bear ravaging your campsite for food. The following is a list of precautions you should take:

1. Keep your food always stored away. Do not leave food out because its scent will travel alerting nearby animals.

CAMPING SURVIVAL HANDBOOK

2. Take your food trash away from your campsite to divert the scent away from your campsite.

3. Do not feed wild animals

4. Don't toy with animals (throwing items at them, etc.)

5. Be harmonious with the animals. They are as much scared of you as you are of them.

CAMPING SURVIVAL HANDBOOK

GENERAL WILDERNESS RULES

- Plan Ahead and Prepare

- Know the regulations and special concerns for the area you'll visit.

- Prepare for extreme weather, hazards, and emergencies.

- Schedule your trip to avoid times of high use.

- Visit in small groups. Split larger parties into smaller groups.

- Repackage food to minimize waste.

- Use a map and compass and never blaze trees, use marking paint, rock cairns or flagging.

- Travel and Camp on Durable Surfaces

- Durable surfaces include established trails and campsites, rock, gravel, dry grasses or snow.

- Obey camping setbacks (100 feet or more) from lakes, streams, trails, other campsites, and historic and cultural sites and structures.

CAMPING SURVIVAL HANDBOOK

- Good campsites are found, not made. Altering a site is not necessary.

In popular areas:
- Concentrate use on existing trails and campsites.

- Walk single file in the middle of the trail, even when wet or muddy.

- Keep campsites small. Focus activity in areas where vegetation is absent.

In pristine areas:
- Disperse use to prevent the creation of campsites and trails.

- Avoid places where impacts are just beginning.

Dispose of Waste Properly
- Pack it in, pack it out. Inspect your campsite and rest areas for trash or spilled foods. Pack out all trash, leftover food, and litter.

- Deposit solid human waste in catholes dug 6 to 8 inches deep at least 200 feet from water, camp, and trails. Cover and disguise the cathole when finished.

- Pack out toilet paper and hygiene products.

CAMPING SURVIVAL HANDBOOK

- To wash yourself or your dishes, carry water 200 feet away from streams or lakes and use small amounts of biodegradable soap. Scatter strained dishwater away from sleeping areas.

Leave What You Find
- Preserve the past: examine, but do not touch, cultural or historic structures and artifacts.

- Leave rocks, plants and other natural objects as you find them.

- Avoid introducing or transporting non-native species.

- Do not build structures, furniture, or dig trenches.

Minimize Campfire Impacts
- Campfires can cause lasting impacts to the backcountry. Instead, consider using a lightweight stove for cooking and a candle lantern for light.

- If fires are permitted, use established fire rings, fire pans, or mound fires.

- Keep fires small. Only use sticks from the ground that can be broken by hand.

CAMPING SURVIVAL HANDBOOK

- Burn all wood and coals to ash, put out campfires completely, then scatter cold ashes.

Respect Wildlife
- Observe wildlife from a distance. Do not follow or approach them.

- Never feed animals. Feeding wildlife damages their health, alters natural behaviors, and exposes them to predators and other dangers.

- Protect wildlife and your food by storing rations and trash securely.

- Control pets at all times, or leave them at home.

- Avoid wildlife during sensitive times: mating, nesting, raising young, or winter.

Be Considerate of Other Visitors
- Respect other visitors and protect the quality of their experience.

- Be courteous. Yield to other users on the trail.

- Step to the downhill side of the trail when encountering horses and pack stock. Stand quietly and speak to riders

CAMPING SURVIVAL HANDBOOK

and horses in a quiet, calm voice to avoid accidents.

- Take breaks and camp away from trails and other visitors.

- Let nature's sounds prevail. Avoid loud voices and noises.

Source: U.S.D.A.

CAMPING SURVIVAL HANDBOOK

ANIMAL TRACKS

CAMPING SURVIVAL HANDBOOK

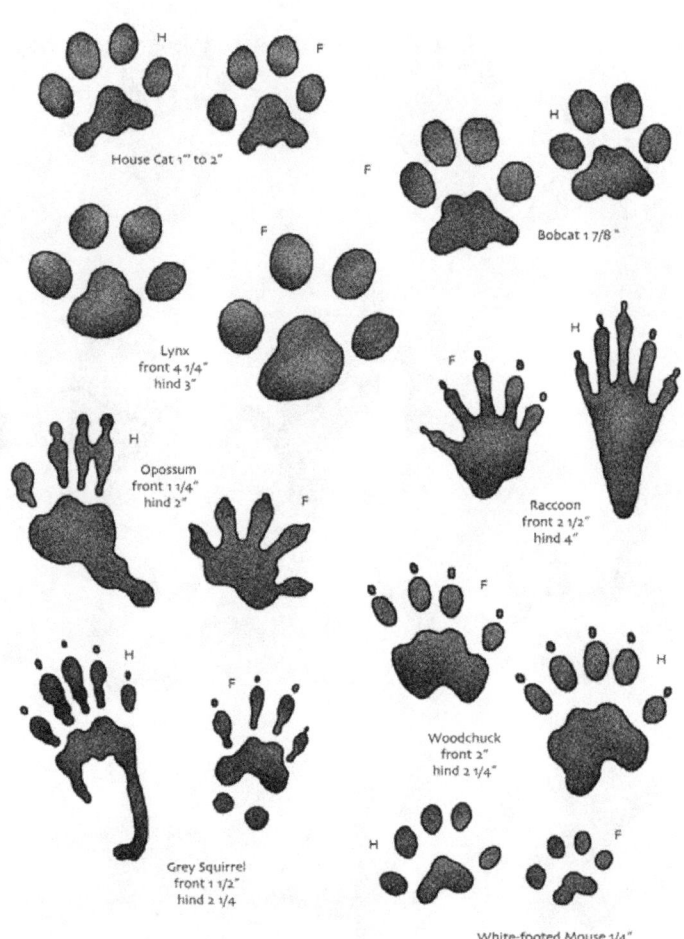

CAMPING SURVIVAL HANDBOOK

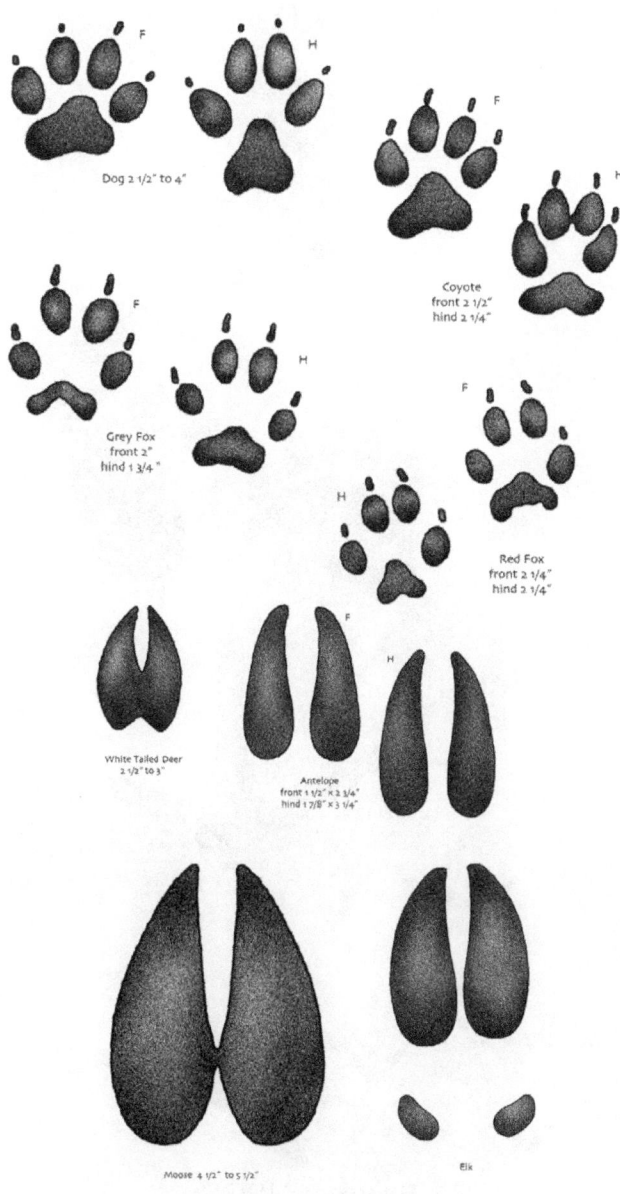

CAMPING SURVIVAL HANDBOOK

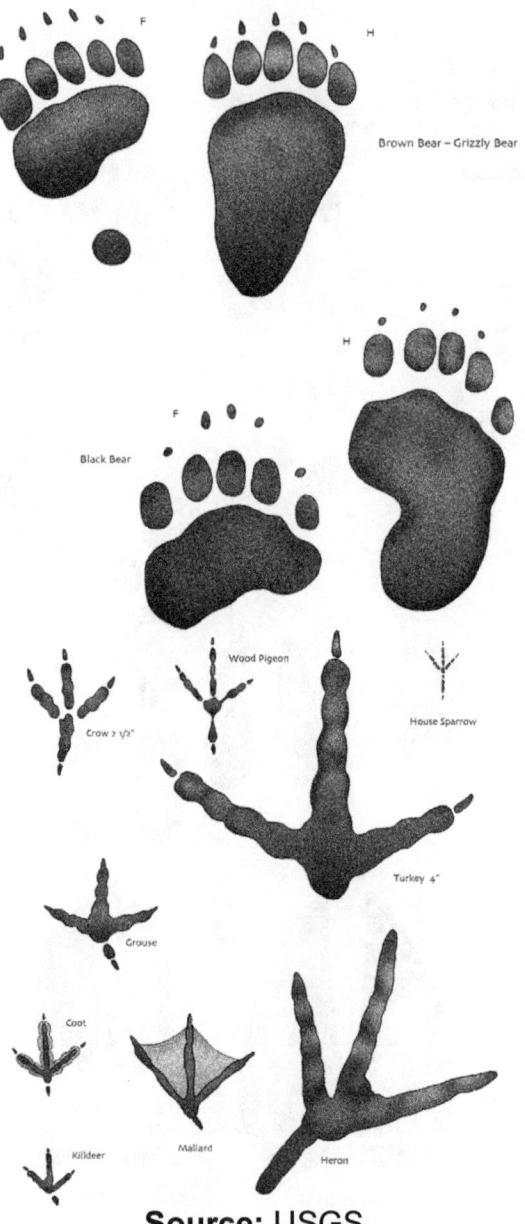

Source: USGS

CAMPING SURVIVAL HANDBOOK

DRAW A MAP
By drawing a map you can know where your campsite is as well as where other notable locations are around you.

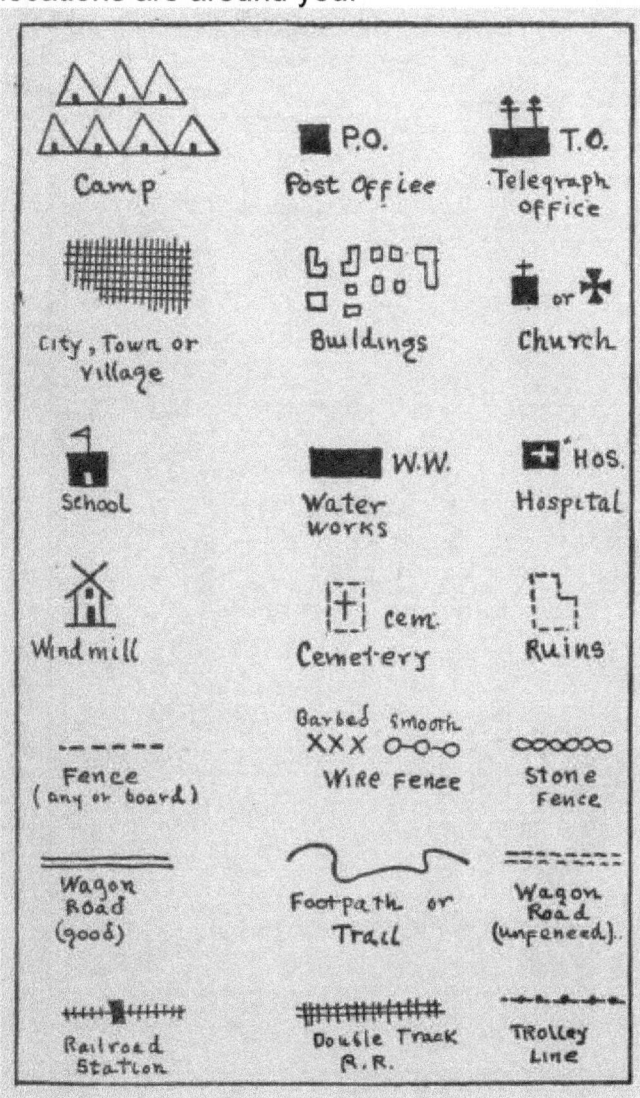

CAMPING SURVIVAL HANDBOOK

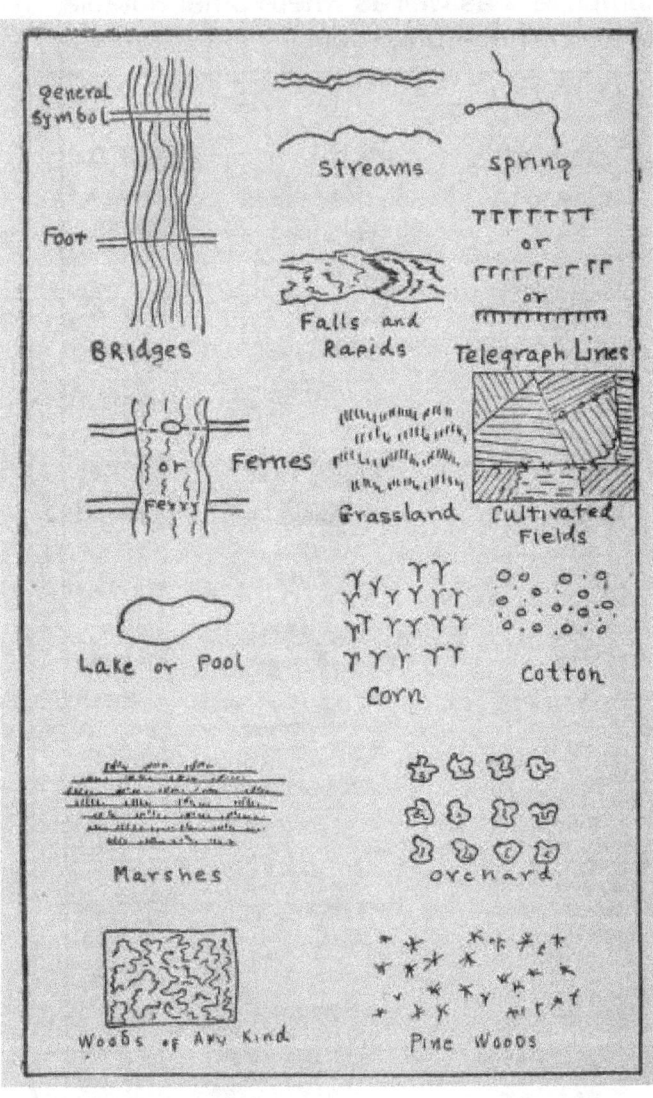

CAMPING SURVIVAL HANDBOOK

MAKING KNOTS
The ability to tie a knot will be useful many times to you for the following purposes:
1. Hauling wood or other objects

2. Lifting an object

3. Climbing or traversing an object.

Bowline Knot

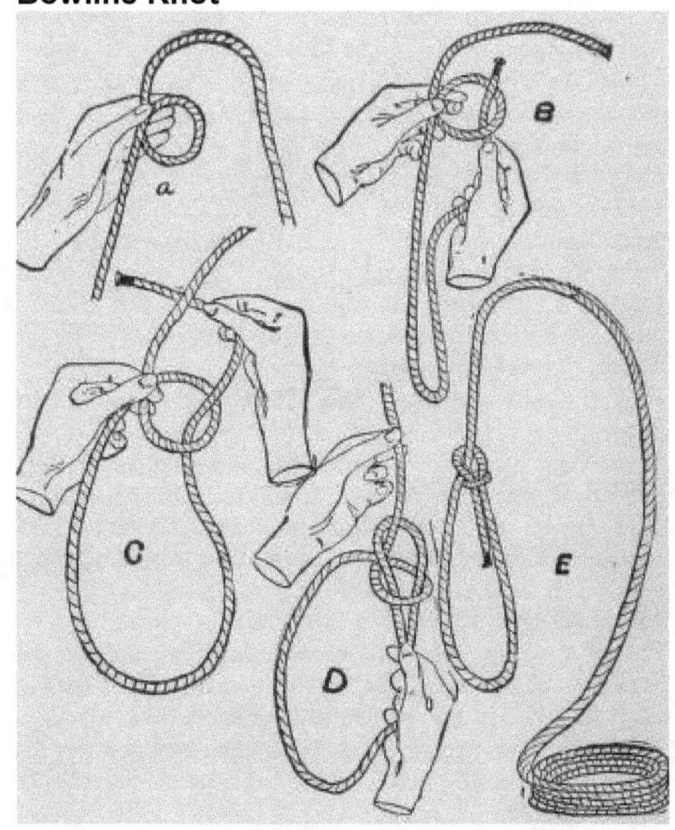

CAMPING SURVIVAL HANDBOOK

Square Knot (Reef)

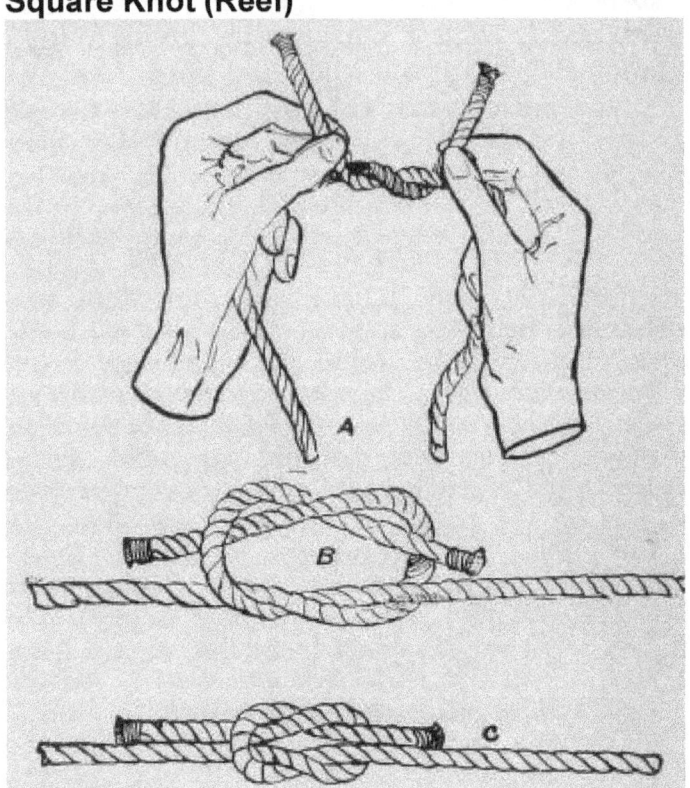

Sheep Shank Knot

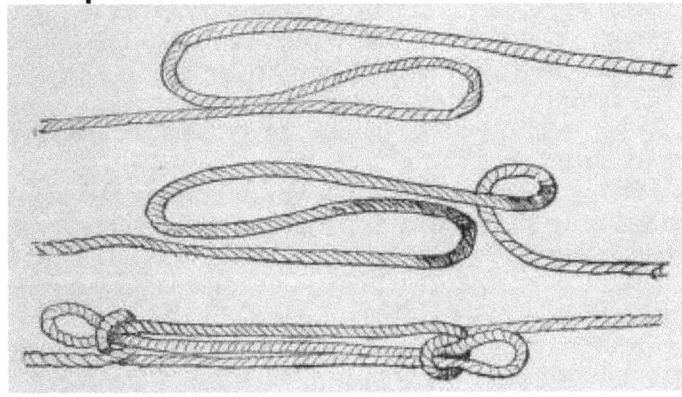

CAMPING SURVIVAL HANDBOOK

Clove Hitch Knot

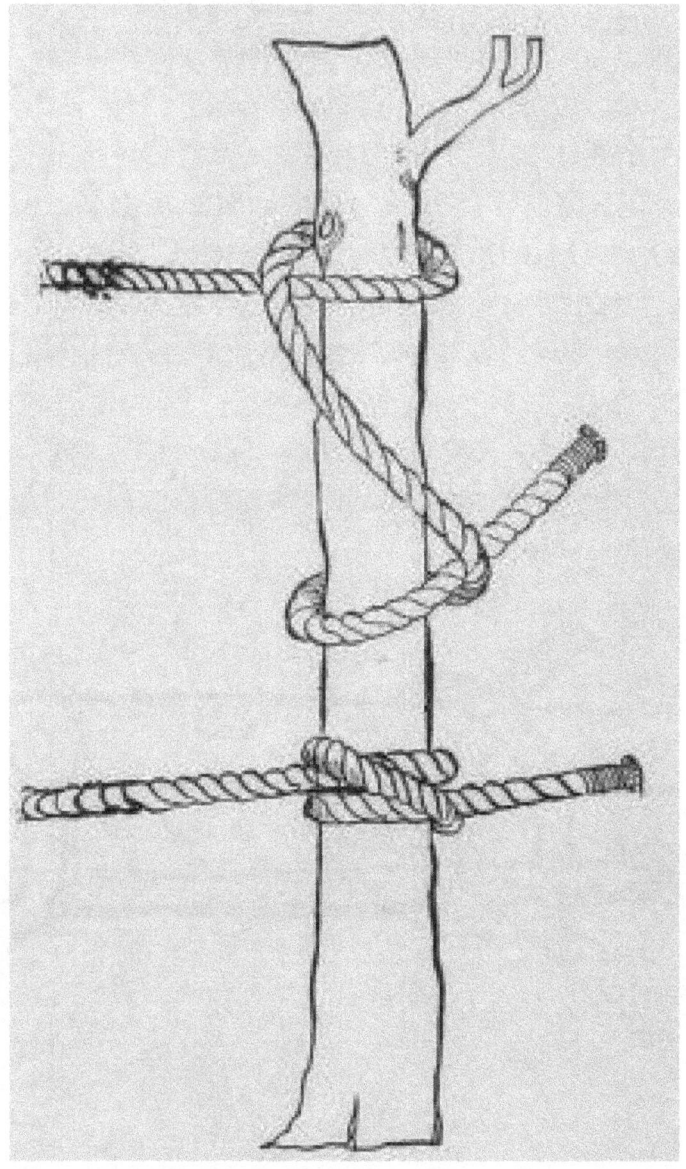

CAMPING SURVIVAL HANDBOOK

NOTES

CAMPING SURVIVAL HANDBOOK

NOTES

CAMPING SURVIVAL HANDBOOK

NOTES

CAMPING SURVIVAL HANDBOOK

NOTES

CAMPING SURVIVAL HANDBOOK

NOTES

CAMPING SURVIVAL HANDBOOK

NOTES

CAMPING SURVIVAL HANDBOOK

NOTES

CAMPING SURVIVAL HANDBOOK

NOTES

… **CAMPING SURVIVAL HANDBOOK**

NOTES

CAMPING SURVIVAL HANDBOOK

NOTES

CAMPING SURVIVAL HANDBOOK

NOTES

CAMPING SURVIVAL HANDBOOK

NOTES

CAMPING SURVIVAL HANDBOOK

NOTES

CAMPING SURVIVAL HANDBOOK

NOTES

CAMPING SURVIVAL HANDBOOK

NOTES

CAMPING SURVIVAL HANDBOOK

NOTES

CAMPING SURVIVAL HANDBOOK

NOTES

CAMPING SURVIVAL HANDBOOK
NOTES

CAMPING SURVIVAL HANDBOOK

NOTES

CAMPING SURVIVAL HANDBOOK

NOTES

CAMPING SURVIVAL HANDBOOK
NOTES

CAMPING SURVIVAL HANDBOOK

NOTES

CAMPING SURVIVAL HANDBOOK

NOTES

CAMPING SURVIVAL HANDBOOK

MIKAZUKI PUBLISHING HOUSE CATALOGUE
Mikazuki Jujitsu Manual
25 Principles of Martial Arts
Karate 360
Political Advertising Manual
Learning Magic
Stories of a Street Performer (Pop Haydn)
Magic as Science & Religion
The Bribe Vibe
World War Water
Small Arms & Deep Pockets
Arctic Black Gold
Find the Ideal Husband
John Locke's 2nd Treatise on Civil Government
The History of Acid Tripping
I Dream In Haiku
Mikazuki Political Science Manual
Tokiwa; A Japanese Love Story
The Card Party; Theater Play
Hagakure; The Book of Hidden Leaves
MMA Coloring Book
DIY Comic Book
Freakshow Los Angeles
Swords & Sails: The Legacy of the Red Lion
Coming to America Handbook
The Medium Writer
California's Next Century 2.0: Economic Renaissance
Self-Examination Diary: Good/Bad Deeds Log
Master Password Organizer Handbook
George Washington's Farewell Address
Customer Profile Organizer

CAMPING SURVIVAL HANDBOOK

United Nations Charter
DIY Comic Book Part II
Storyboard Book: Make Your Movie Series
Basketball Team Play Design Book
Football Play Design Book
T-Shirt Design Book
Rappers Rhyme Book: Lyricists Notebook
Japan History Coloring Book
Magicians Coloring Book
The Adventures of Sherlock Holmes
Words of King Darius
The Art of War
The Book of Five Rings
Tao Te Ching
Captain Bligh's Voyage
Beginner's Magician Manual
The Man that Made the English Language
The Arrival of Palloncino
The Irish Republican Army Manual of Guerrilla Warfare
Living the Pirate Code
Van Carlton Detective Agency; The Burgundy Diamond
Quotes Gone Wild
Shogun X the Last Immortal
The Art of Western Boxing
William Shakespeare's Sonnets
U.S. Military Boxing Manual
Mythology Coloring Book
U.S. Army Anti-Guerrilla Warfare Manual
Boxing Coloring Book
Wild Wilderness Coloring Book

www.ingramcontent.com/pod-product-compliance
Lightning Source LLC
LaVergne TN
LVHW011206080426
835508LV00007B/628